D1104201

Football

The Greatest Moments in the Southwest Conference

FOOTBALL

The Greatest Moments in the Southwest Conference

by WILL GRIMSLEY

LITTLE, BROWN AND COMPANY · BOSTON · TORONTO

COPYRIGHT © 1968 BY WILL GRIMSLEY
ALL RIGHTS RESERVED. NO PART OF THIS BOOK MAY BE REPRODUCED
IN ANY FORM OR BY ANY ELECTRONIC OR MECHANICAL MEANS IN-
CLUDING INFORMATION STORAGE AND RETRIEVAL SYSTEMS WITHOUT
PERMISSION IN WRITING FROM THE PUBLISHER, EXCEPT BY A REVIEWER
WHO MAY QUOTE BRIEF PASSAGES IN A REVIEW.
LIBRARY OF CONGRESS CATALOG CARD NO. 68-30870
FIRST EDITION

PHOTOGRAPH CREDITS

Numbers refer to pages on which pictures may be found

LAUGHEAD PHOTOGRAPHERS: 3, 6, 9, 10, 12, 13, 22, 23, 33, 38, 43, 44, 48, 52, 56, 58, 59, 65, 66, 73, 74, 75, 79, 82, 83, 84, 85, 86, 89, 93, 109, 116, 122, 132, 133, 134

WIDE WORLD PHOTOS: 5, 16, 17, 18, 31, 37, 39, 62, 87, 91, 94, 104, 117, 119, 124

AP WIRE PHOTO: 136, 147, 149, 150, 152

FORT WORTH STAR TELEGRAM: iii, 64, 69, 96, 103

LARRY OBSITNIK: 126, 140, 141, 143

HAROLD KEITH: iv, 107

BAGBY PHOTO CO.: 67

TEXAS CHRISTIAN UNIVERSITY: 101

GENE PRESCOTT: 139

*Published simultaneously in Canada
by Little, Brown & Company (Canada) Limited*
PRINTED IN THE UNITED STATES OF AMERICA

Contents

71-4502

PULASKI-PERRY REG. LIBRARY
LITTLE ROCK, ARKANSAS

Acknowledgments

It is impossible to produce a book of this kind without drawing upon the research of other historians, the recollections of writers who covered the games, the reminiscences of the players who lived them and those hardworking college publicists whose job it is to give the drama and its actors the fullest exposure. To all of these, I am indebted for their help in composing this modest effort to whip up some of the cream of a football-mad area.

Special credit goes to authors of books on the subject. These include Allison Danzig, *The History of American Football;* Harold V. Ratliff, *The Power and the Glory;* Kern Tips, *Football Texas Style;* J. W. Williams, *Sizzling Southwest;* Fred Russell and George Leonard, *Big Bowl Football;* Darrell Royal and Blackie Sherrod, *Darrell Royal Talks Football,* and Dave Campbell, editor of *Texas Football* magazine.

My thanks also to the sportswriters who covered the games on the spot, including Dan Jenkins, *Sports Illustrated;* Blackie Sherrod, Dallas *Times Herald;* Sam Blair, Dallas *Morning News;* Dick Peebles; Houston *Chronicle;* Mickey Herskowitz, Houston *Post;* Bob Rule, formerly of the Houston *Press;* Harold V. Ratliff, B. M. Kellum and Max Skelton, The Associated Press; Orville Henry and Orville Henry, Jr., Little Rock *Arkansas Gazette.*

Tremendous help was given by the following college sports publicity directors: Wilbur Evans, Southwest Conference; George Wright, Baylor; Bill Whitmore, Rice; F. F. (Junior) Eldredge, Southern Methodist; Bill Holmes and Bob Condron, Texas Tech; Jim Brock, Texas Christian; H. L. (Spec) Gammon, Texas A&M; Jones Ramsey, University of Texas; Bob Cheyne, Arkansas; Harold Keith, University of Oklahoma; Bill Callahan, University of Missouri; Roger Valdiserri, Notre Dame; and Bud Thalman, U.S. Naval Academy.

I am indebted to those coaches and players who took time off from busy schedules to relate incidents and anecdotes surrounding the games. These include Paul (Bear) Bryant, Alabama; Gene Stallings, Texas A&M; Darrell Royal, Texas; Bud Wilkinson, Oklahoma; Matty Bell, Southern Methodist; Dutch Meyer, Texas Christian; J. T. King, Texas Tech; Kyle Rote and Doak Walker, Southern Methodist; Bobby Layne, Texas; and Donny Anderson, Texas Tech.

My deepest gratitude also to all the kindly ladies in newspaper offices and libraries across the land who always were most courteous in producing microfilm and assisting in operation of the machines.

It is impossible to repay these kindnesses in kind.

WILL GRIMSLEY

Football
The Greatest Moments
in the Southwest
Conference

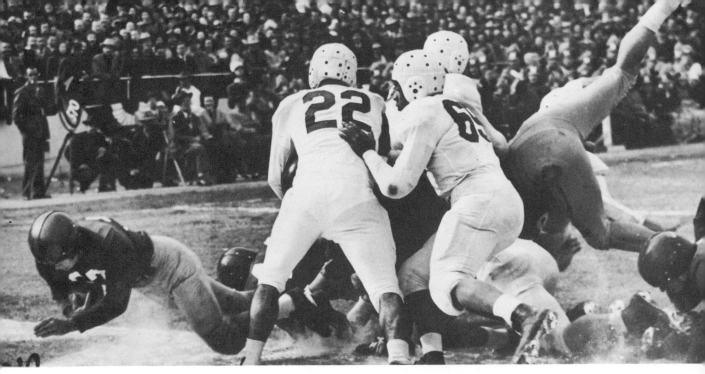

Hard action in the Cotton Bowl: Doak Walker scores and Floyd McKissick's legs go flying

Prologue

In 1935, when Matty Bell inherited the head coaching job at Southern Methodist University from Ray Morrison, who was returning to his alma mater Vanderbilt, he found himself in the midst of a wild circus.

"All the players were running around yelling 'cow cow,'" Bell explained later. "The center would snap the ball to a halfback, and you'd think he had caught a red-hot flatiron. He would holler 'cow cow' and lateral it off to another back, who would yell 'cow cow' and throw it to somebody else. Every time a man was tackled, he would give out with that 'cow cow' stuff and get rid of the ball. It was really crazy."

Crazy or not, the SMU team, which Bell took over from Morrison, won twelve straight games, became recognized as the national champion and went to the Rose Bowl — the first team from west of the Mississippi River to be so honored. It was then — and not until then — that the rest of the country took note of Southwest Conference football.

Up to that time, a cloak of virtual anonymity had shrouded the Texas game, which was as wild and wide open as the cowboy country itself.

Teams were traditionally small and leather-tough — 165-pounders being the rule rather than the 200-pound behemoths making headlines in the East and the developing Middle West. They played a risky, gambling style of football, always shooting from the hip and to blazes with the defense. In earlier days, this same SMU had been beaten 146–3 by Rice. But it had gone down gloriously, trying to the end for the long "bomb."

College football historians haven't reached complete agreement on who threw the first successful overhand forward pass, or where the historic deed took place. Both the East and Texas take credit for utilizing the pass as an offensive weapon — as does the Notre Dame team of 1913, with Gus Dorais at quarterback and Knute Rockne at end, in its astounding 35–13 victory over a massive and heavily favored Army. But few deny that it was in the arid Southwest that the forward pass found its true habitat — to be used and nurtured and exploited for decades of exciting, unpredictable football.

Principal architect of this uninhibited brand of attack was Morrison, a scholarly, soft-spoken former Vanderbilt quarterback who doubled as a mathematics professor. Shortly after becoming head coach at SMU a second time in 1922, he spawned what became nationally known as the Aerial Circus. Another name for it was "razzle-dazzle." The ball seemed to be in the air so much it was a wonder it didn't die of pneumonia, and the players grabbed it and got rid of it as if it singed their fingers. To the opposition and to the spectator, it was difficult to tell whether it was open-field basketball or sleight-of-hand.

At any rate it was successful, and SMU's Aerial Circus produced Conference championships in 1923 and 1927. Other Southwest teams became infected with the razzle-dazzle bug and the epidemic spread throughout the Conference. Wide-open football became the Conference trademark. Southwest teams, with their Sammy Baughs, John Kimbroughs, Bobby Laynes, Doak Walkers and Kyle Rotes, moved to the front of the national picture. If Southwesterners suffered in national ratings, the reason could be traced to their own backyard. Competition was so fierce and unpredictable that the teams were constantly knocking each other off the pedestal.

The first organized college team in the Southwest was the University of Texas. The date was 1893 — fourteen years after the historic battle between Rutgers and Princeton at New Brunswick, New Jersey, on November 6, 1869, the first intercollegiate football game played in the United States.

The Texas team was a scrawny band of students — exactly eleven of them in all, whose coach as shown in the early tintypes was a man

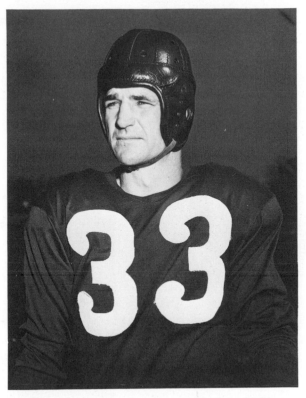

Washington Redskin, Sam Baugh, photographed in 1945, ten years after "the game of the year," when SMU beat TCU on its way to the Rose Bowl

named Crawford with brilliant tinted black hair, parted in the middle, a snappy bow tie and a black, funeral-parlor suit. The players wore laced moleskin uniforms, without padding, and high black stockings. Instead of headgear, they had small beanies, principally to keep their flowing hair out of their eyes.

The game was a mixture of rugby and soccer, with soccer rules largely prevailing. The field was marked off in checkerboard squares. The length of the game was ninety minutes, with forty-five-minute halves. Touchdowns counted four points, conversions two.

In its first year, the Texas Varsity — as it so proudly called itself — had to be content to play informal games around Austin with independent town teams. It was not until the next year, 1894, that intercollegiate football was born in the Southwest.

The place was Clark Field in Austin. The antagonists were Texas and the newly organized team representing Texas A&M. It was a crisp October day and word of the big conflict had spread throughout the area. A goodly crowd, highly excited, was on the sidelines, mostly

Dana X. Bible, the immortal Longhorn mentor as he receives his
award at the Texas Hall of Fame

LEFT TO RIGHT: *D. X. Bible, Texas; Fred Thomsen, Arkansas;*
Matty Bell, SMU; Homer Norton, Texas A&M; Dutch Meyer, TCU

Ray Morrison, one of the Conference's
great coaches while at SMU receives the
Hall of Fame Award from Gerald Mann

students. The men were dapper in their short coats, tight trousers and bowler hats. The co-eds giggled under wide-brimmed hats with veils tied beneath their chins. Their blouses had leg-of-mutton sleeves and their skirts dipped to the tops of their high-button shoes. But they moved up and down the field with the ball and cheered wildly every time their heroes came together with a bone-rattling thud.

Texas won the game, 38–0, with eight touchdowns and three conversions (all dropkicks) and became so cocky that it sent a letter to the newly formed team of the University of Arkansas, challenging the boys from the Ozarks to a contest at Austin.

Arkansas accepted. It little mattered that the trip from Fayetteville by rail and carriage took six days and that the Cardinals, as they termed themselves, were so exhausted by the time the game was played on Thanksgiving Day that they were easy victims, 54–0. Yet in the space of a few weeks in 1894 were born two series which were to become the most colorful and hardest fought in the decades to follow.

In the space of three years, football had become a thriving sport at the large state universities — Texas, Texas A&M, Arkansas and Oklahoma — and interest was being pricked at the budding denominational institutions. AddRan College in Fort Worth, named for Addison and Randolph Clark, joined the parade in 1896. Baylor, backed by the Baptists, fielded its first team in 1899. AddRan, supported by the Disciples of Christ, changed its name to Texas Christian University in 1902.

The game was not confined to the bigger universities. During the late 1890s and early 1900s, teams cropped up at Austin College, Trinity, Hardin-Simmons, Daniel Baker (later merged with Howard Payne), St. Edwards and Southwestern. With smaller student bodies to draw from, these schools nevertheless fielded representative squads that often spoiled the records of the powers of the day.

With a limited number of teams, Southwest colleges often found it necessary to play the same rival two or three times in a single season to complete a schedule. Baylor and Texas A&M, for example, clashed three times in 1901. The games were largely informal — each side having its own scorekeeper — and disputes arose over who was the winner.

In the 1901 Baylor–Aggie series, for instance, Baylor contends it won two games and tied the third, 6–6. The Aggies, disputing a Baylor touchdown and conversion, recorded it as a 6–0 Texas A&M victory. A simple dispute arose over a Baylor–Texas Christian game in 1907, and the athletic archives of the two institutions have it two different ways. TCU contends it won 11–0 and Baylor has it listed 10–9 in favor of the Bears. It so happens that even the officials on the field that day couldn't agree on a controversial safety. The goal lines were virtually obliterated by the dusty scrambling. TCU contended it tackled a Baylor ballcarrier in the Baylor end zone. Baylor said it wasn't so. With the officials also divided, there was no one to verify what actually happened.

Records of the era are fragmentary. However, one of them states that Texas was the scene of the first touchdown pass ever thrown in college football. The year was said to be 1906. The game involved Texas and Texas A&M Winston McMahon lobbed a pass to Bowie Duncan in helping Texas to a 24–0 victory. Eastern historians dispute this claim. They say the first forward pass for a touchdown was thrown by Sammy Moore of Wesleyan University of Connecticut against Yale. It soared 18 yards into the hands of Irvin Van Tassell, who proceeded over the goal line. The year was also 1906, but the Eastern historians cite a precise date of October 3.

Controversies were rampant in the swaddling years of Southwest football, and few them were ever settled to everybody's satisfaction.

There was the case of Baylor's "quick switch" in 1908. The Baptists had already lost two games to Texas Christian and were seeking some sort of revenge in a third meeting at Waco, Texas, on Thanksgiving Day. But the game took the trend of the previous encounters and the Christians led 8–6 at the half.

For the Baptists, this called for desperate measures. So during the half, Baylor, with the aid and connivance of both the coach and captain, cooked up a diabolical scheme. John Flouts, the star Baylor end, changed from Baylor's gray to TCU's blue stockings but kept on his gray jersey. After the kickoff, however, he rushed to the sidelines and donned a blue jersey such as that worn by the TCU team, so that he looked like a twelfth man on the field for the Christians.

The TCU team was thrown into a state of complete befuddlement. It protested to the officials. But Baylor's captain, Babe Gantt, said there was no rule against it, and there wasn't. Out of the chaos and confusion, Baylor emerged with a 23–8 come-from-behind triumph that sent the town of Waco into wild hysterics. TCU chose never to record the game. Baylor did.

The bitterness on both sides was almost as keen after a 1910 game between Baylor and Texas which Baylor called a 6–6 tie and Texas listed a 1–0 Longhorn victory by default. The Golden Bears of Baylor had gone into the game with an unbeaten record, but the powerful Texans were heavily favored. For three-fourths of the game the two teams battled furiously, with neither gaining a dominant edge. With the score 6–6 late in the second half, there was a controversial play.

All-American Joe Routt of Texas A&M, 1936

The official ruled in favor of Texas. Baylor Coach Ralph Glaze, a former end at Dartmouth, became so incensed that he bundled up his players and took them off the field. The game was listed officially as a forfeit, but Baylor never recognized the decision.

It became quite evident after a while that such madcap disorganized competition could not continue. Otherwise, it was feared, some of the players might start bringing six-shooters onto the field, as one player, a rangy guard named Ed (Cowboy) Bull of AddRan College, once threatened to do. "I always wear my shootin' iron when I'm among strangers," Bull told a teammate as he rammed a Colt into his belt. He was dissuaded from carrying it onto the field against Texas.

It was obvious that football in the Southwest needed some sort of direction, so a move was begun in 1914 to form a conference which would govern the competition. The Southwest Conference emerged a year later.

The Southwest Conference began producing dramatic football from the day of its formal organization in 1915, although scheduling was on a catch-as-catch-can basis and its games attracted little notice outside its own confines.

The first year, a game between Oklahoma and Texas produced a total of seventy-one passes — an unheard-of number for that rather conservative era — but most of them fell through slippery fingers. Oklahoma won the game only 14–13. Spot Geyer was the pitcher for the Sooners and Clyde Littlefield did the passing for the Longhorns.

It was ironic that the Southwest continued its failure to attract national attention even when Dana Zenephon Bible moved to Texas A&M as head coach in 1917 and launched a football dynasty that saw the Aggies rack up two perfect seasons in which they were unbeaten, untied and unscored-on. The so-called farmer boys from College Station had a string of eighteen games in which they scored 516 points to none for the opposition.

D. X. Bible was a graduate of Carson-Newman College in Tennessee. He coached at Mississippi College and Louisiana State before launching his big-time coaching career at Texas A&M. A dapper man, almost bald at twenty-five when he inherited the Aggies, Bible went on to become one of the game's legendary tacticians. He coached for thirty-four years, twenty-nine of them at Texas A&M, the remainder at Nebraska and Texas, and fourteen of his teams won conference championships. They called him The Little General.

Bible's early Aggie teams produced some of the conference's immortals. Rip Collins was the first of his great punters, averaging around 50 yards. Arthur Knickerbocker and Abe (Bugs) Morris were quarterbacks. Jack Mahan was a crunching fullback.

The Aggies' winning streak under Bible was brought to an end on Thanksgiving Day, 1920, by Texas; and one of the chief architects of the Longhorns' upset triumph was a nimble-foot athlete named Kyle

Explosive Aggie back Dick Todd, 1936–37   *Jack Wilson of Baylor, 1937*

(Slippery) Elam, who had contributed to the Aggies' success in previous years.

Elam played safety on the 1917 Texas A&M team and is credited with saving a 7–0 victory over Baylor by making a flying tackle of a Baylor receiver who was racing for what looked to be a sure touchdown. Under the loose Conference transfer rules, Elam shifted to Texas where he was to become quarterback of the team that succeeded the Aggies as Conference champions.

In that fabled 1920 game, last of the season, the Aggies outplayed Texas for more than three periods and were leading 3–0 midway of the fourth period. Then Elam called a crisscross play that mesmerized a crowd of 18,300 — the largest turnout to see a Southwest football game up to that time — and cracked one of the most fantastic winning strings fashioned in college football. Starting with the last game in 1918, the Aggies had swept through eighteen straight games without yielding a point.

The Longhorns had moved to the Aggie's 11-yard line but there the Aggie defense, led by tackles Dunny McMurray and Ox Ford, guards Woodrow Wilson and Cap Murrah and ends Tim Griesenbeck and Puny Wilson, threw back three straight Texas thrusts at the line.

Elam's razzle-dazzle play came on last down. Francisco Domingues took the ball from center Swede Swenson and handed the ball off to Jack Barry. The latter flipped a pass to a tackle, Tom Dennis, who had become an eligible receiver when the end peeled off just before the snap and took position at the opposite end. Dennis made a leaping, one-hand catch of the ball, thrown almost laterally across the field and he fell under a horde of Aggies on the five-yard line. Domingues crashed over from the five for the touchdown and the extra point gave Texas a historic 7–3 triumph. The Longhorns were destined to go on to thirteen Conference championships, won outright or shared, and to produce some of the finest players and greatest moments of the game.

But the wily D. X. Bible was far from finished. He brought his Aggies back the following season, 1921, to regain the league crown. Then he took part in the first post-season game played in the South, a spectacle called the Dixie Bowl and a forerunner of the Cotton Bowl.

It was played January 2, 1922, in Dallas. The principals were Texas A&M and the famed Praying Colonels of Little Centre College in Kentucky. Centre, coached by Charley Moran and quarterbacked by Bo McMillin, had become a national legend. Composed largely of Texans from the Fort Worth area, the Praying Colonels had been traveling throughout the country, whipping the top football powers of the day. One of their victims had been a powerful Harvard team.

The game was played in connection with the Texas State Fair at Fair Park. The Praying Colonels, overwhelmingly favored, apparently took the game too lightly. McMillin, himself a Texan, strode onto the field with his bride of a day on his arm. Moran, a former Texas League football player and later an outstanding umpire, made no effort to fire up his barnstorming giant-killers.

Puny Wilson recalled later that Bible had called the team together before the game and made a very short but effective talk. "We were ready," Wilson said.

Wilson, Cap Murrah, Sammy Sanders, Ted Winn and others swarmed all over McMillin. It was the 1922 version of the "blitz," made famous later in professional football. Wilson was shifted to the backfield. Passing and running, he led the Aggies to a 22–14 triumph. It was the first of many bowl successes for the Southwest Conference.

It was in this game that the Aggies' "Twelfth Man" tradition was born. As the game progressed, one after another of the Aggies' ball-carriers went out with injuries. Heinie Weir suffered a broken leg in the first period. Another halfback went out with a twisted knee. Another sprained an ankle. Soon there were no halfback substitutes on the Aggie bench.

Bible became desperate. Suddenly he remembered that a former squad member, King Gill, was in the stands with the uniformed Cadet Corps. Gill had been on the football squad until Thanksgiving Day, when he left to practice basketball. The A&M coach sent word into the stands that Gill was wanted on the Aggie bench — dressed and ready to play. Gill responded. It is immaterial that his services were never needed and he never got into action. From that day on, the

Jack Robb
passer, 19.

Baylor players take their mascot to practice with his birthday cake

kansas's great

Cadet Corps made a practice of standing at every game, letting the coach know that any member was ready for service if needed.

The Aggies' chief rivals for conference honors in the 1920s were Southern Methodist, where Vanderbilt's Ray Morrison had unfurled his Aerial Circus, and Baylor, which had its finest days under a tough little Harvard graduate named Frank Bridges.

Baylor beat the Aggies 13–7 in 1922 — the Bears' third victory over A&M in twenty-two years — and went on to win the championship. Ten players went the full sixty minutes for the Bears. Only twelve men got into the Baylor lineup, the lone substitution being Ox Fullingham for Hankshaw Crosby at one end when the latter was injured.

Bridges was an inventor of gadgets and unusual maneuvers which kept his opposition in a constant dither and the rules makers in a state of confusion. Well within the rules at the time, he conceived a chest harness for his linemen. The linemen would grasp the harness with their hands, forcing their elbows wide. Together, they formed a wedge for offensive blocking. The harness later was banned.

One of Bridges' most effective plays was a hidden-ball trick which he called the "tackle around." For this, he needed a tackle who could also carry the ball and he found him in Russell Blailock, a rugged boy from Waco, Texas, who blocked viciously and ran like a fullback. On the play, the quarterback, just behind the center, would fake as if he had received the ball and scoot around one end behind a wave of blockers. The opposition and officials usually went with him. But he didn't have the ball at all. Instead, the ball had been jammed by the center under the legs of a squatting guard, who hovered over it like a mother hen. When the play had moved sufficiently in the right direction, the tackle — in this case, Blailock — would make a block and

Ends Ray Hamilton and Jim Benton of Arkansas, 1936–37

All-American Dick Harris of Texas, 1947

then move over to the guard, wresting the ball from beneath his legs and taking off downfield, usually alone, for a touchdown.

During this same period, Rice Institute imported a "big-name" coach, John Heisman, whose name later was to grace the trophy given yearly to the outstanding college player. Heisman had built a national reputation as a strategist and innovator, being credited with the so-called Heisman shift, the center snapback and the plan of calling signals at the line of scrimmage. The coaching pioneer enjoyed less than moderate success during his four years at Rice, starting in 1924, but he made his mark on the Conference.

At Southern Methodist, Coach Ray Morrison always seemed to come up with a slick, sharp-throwing quarterback. One of the best was Logan Stollenwerck, who carried the Mustangs through a nine-game season in 1923 in which the opposition scored a total of only nine points. Stollenwerck's passing helped beat Arkansas, a team on which SMU had never scored before, 13–6, and then smash Texas A&M in the final game, 16–0. Baylor won league titles in 1922 and 1924, SMU in 1923 and 1926, Texas A&M in 1925 and 1927.

The three campaigns covering 1925, 1926 and 1927 featured a personal quarterback duel between two of the smallest and cleverest field generals ever to play in the Southwest. They were Joel Hunt, a 145-pound triple threat from Waco, Texas, who showed up at Texas A&M unannounced and battled his way to a varsity spot on the football team, and Gerald (Jerry) Mann, a 150-pound broken field runner and passer who played for Southern Methodist.

They squared off as sophomores in 1925, neither with much fanfare, and Hunt drew first blood, although there was little to choose between the performances. After a scoreless first half, Hunt led the Aggies to a touchdown in the third period, scoring on a 12-yard pass to Fay (Mule) Wilson, kid brother of Puny Wilson. Mann led a comeback surge by SMU which carried to the edge of the A&M goal only to be stopped when time ran out. A&M won, 7–0.

Mann evened the score the next year when the Mustangs and Aggies met at Dallas in their opening Conference game of the campaign. Hunt got A&M off to a quick lead with a fourth-down touchdown pass to Jelly Woodman but Mann rallied with a thirty-yard scoring pass to fullback Howard Wade and a field goal which gave SMU a 9–7 victory, the start of an unbeaten and championship season.

Hunt played one of his greatest games in the "rubber match" with his Mustang rival in 1927, the Aggies winning 39–13.

Southern Methodist came into the game unbeaten but it found Hunt thirsting for revenge. The little Aggie all-purpose back dominated the game. He scored three touchdowns and passed for a fourth. He intercepted four of Mann's passes, punted for an average of more than forty yards and played both offense and defense. He missed only three minutes of action during the season.

He kicked off, did all the team's punting and place-kicking, passed, ran the ball three out of four times, called signals and served as team captain. He scored 128 points in his final season, setting a Conference record.

Bible called Hunt one of the most talented players he ever coached, and another observer said of the Aggie pony back: "A flaming spirit drove Hunt to greatness. He was a natural player. He liked practice. He loved to scrimmage. He possessed an ability that led a contemporary to muse, 'He ain't so fast, but you couldn't catch him in a telephone booth.' "

With all his greatness, Hunt found one nemesis during his three seasons at Texas A&M. He was Raymond (Rags) Matthews, a fierce 185-pounder who played end for Texas Christian Horned Frogs. Hunt was never able to beat a TCU team. During the coinciding varsity careers of Hunt and Matthews, Texas Christian had a victory and two ties against the Aggies.

Matthews got his nickname in high school at Fort Worth because his jersey was always being torn off in fights. Some have acclaimed him the best defensive player ever to come out of the Southwest. In the 1927 East-West game at San Francisco, Matthews hit Glenn Presnell, the touted Nebraska back, so hard on the first play that Presnell fumbled and left the field with a cracked collarbone. It was in the same game that the tough TCU end, according to legend, openly challenged Bruce Caldwell, the Yale ace playing on the East team.

"Hey, Mister Caldwell," Matthews reportedly yelled out to Caldwell, "how come you don't try an end run this way? Come on around my end, suh." The Yale All-American five times accepted the taunt and never gained an inch.

Matthews played without a headgear. He was rated the fastest man in football for the first ten yards — in other words, he had amazing "torque." Although renowned for his defensive play, he also was a good pass receiver. In a 1926 game against Southern Methodist he caught eight passes out of eight for 110 yards.

Matthews' private target, however, seemed to be Joel Hunt, whose backfield exploits had made him the talk of the Conference.

In the 1927 game, Texas A&M drove to the TCU one-yard line with four tries to make a touchdown. Mainly because of the charging defensive play of Matthews, the Aggies wound up on the five. Most

Southwest coaches gave orders to their teams never to run to Matthews' side.

Because Southwest football had not yet gained full recognition, neither Mann, Hunt nor Matthews ever made All-American.

The first official All-American in the Southwest Conference was a strapping Arkansas end named Wear Schoonover. Schoonover began his career under the colorful Francis Schmidt, who later moved to Texas Christian. The Arkansas end produced credentials in the 1929 season that could not be denied. He played every minute of every game in a rugged nine-game schedule. He caught seven touchdown passes and scored fifty-four points. Against Baylor he grabbed fourteen of seventeen passes. He caught two passes that set up touchdowns in the Texas A&M game and blocked the extra point try that gave Arkansas a 14–13 victory. He intercepted five passes against Centenary and ran one of them back 92 yards for a score.

In 1930, the Southwest placed another player on virtually every All-American team — Bochey Koch, a powerful, thick-necked Baylor guard. Koch was so aggressive in the Dixie Classic post-season game against Purdue — a prelude to the Cotton Bowl — that one of the Boilermaker backs complained that he didn't play on the line as he was supposed to, but played in the Purdue backfield.

Southwest teams also began attracting more attention by increasing their intersectional schedules and one of the most ambitious of these was Ray Morrison's Aerial Circus from SMU. Southern Methodist, with one of its better teams, invaded South Bend, Indiana, in 1930 for a confrontation with Knute Rockne's Fighting Irish of Notre Dame, then rated No. 1 in the country.

This was the Notre Dame team that had Frank Carideo, two-time All-

Coach Jess Neely of Rice with three star performers: King Hill (kneeling), Frank Ryan and Buddy Dial 1957

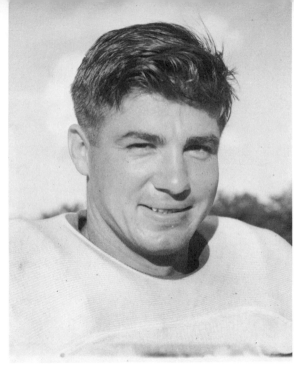

Pete Layden,
Texas All-American
quarterback, 1941

American, at quarterback; Marchie Schwartz; Marty Brill; and the 153-pound watchfob guard, Bert Metzger. Notre Dame was expected to make mincemeat of the lean, hungry Texans from SMU although it was known that the Methodists kept the air filled with footballs.

The Methodists proved a surprise. Led by Weldon (Speedy) Mason, the Mustangs confused the Irish by throwing the ball around as if it were a hot flatiron and no one was more surprised than the great Rockne when the teams went to their locker rooms at the half with the score tied 14–14. In the third period, the Mustangs got a bad break when they had a pass interference penalty called against them which gave Notre Dame the ball on the SMU four-yard line. Schwartz plowed across for the touchdown but the pressure of SMU's rush resulted in a miss in the try for extra point. Notre Dame led 20–14.

The missed conversion began to take on huge proportions late in the game when the Mustangs launched a drive that had the Irish reeling. With Bob Gilbert hitting his receivers and Speedy Mason spinning off short gains, SMU drove from its own 6-yard line to the Notre Dame forty-three. With time fast running out, Gilbert arched a long desperation pass to Mason on the Notre Dame goal line. There was a tense moment on the Irish bench but Tommy Yarr of Notre Dame rushed up to make an interception. The Irish held on for a 20–14 victory, one of ten straight which made them national champions for the second consecutive year.

Nineteen years later another Notre Dame championship team received an even greater scare from SMU in a game at Dallas, but that is a chapter in itself.

*Don Meredith
of SMU, 1958*

*One of the game's
greatest linebackers:
Tommy Nobis of Texas*

With the start of the 1930s, the University of Texas, under Coach Clyde Littlefield, moved back to front and center. Spearheads of the team were a talented twosome named Ernie Koy and Harrison Stafford. Koy, whose son by the same name was to follow in his footsteps, was both a passer and a runner. Stafford was an excellent ballcarrier and receiver. During the three varsity years of Koy and Stafford, 1930–1932, the Longhorns won twenty-four games, lost only six and tied none. They were Conference champions in 1930.

By the middle and late 1930s, football fans in New York, Detroit, Denver and Los Angeles were getting a steady diet of the individual and team heroics in the wide-open Southwest. Texas football had proved it belonged.

Texas Christian turned up with a trigger-armed passer named Sammy Baugh, one of the greatest passers the game has yet to know, and followed him with a dazzling little guy named Davey O'Brien. Rice had a pair of racehorse backs in Ernie Lain and Olie Cordill. There also were Bobby Wilson of Southern Methodist, Billy Patterson of Baylor and big John Kimbrough of Texas A&M.

Samuel Adrian Baugh played high school football in Sweetwater, Texas. He tried to get into several big name football schools after graduation but none was very interested. So Sammy cast his lot with TCU, where as a freshman in 1934 he fell under the wing of Coach Dutch Meyer. Meyer, destined to lead the Horned Frogs for eighteen years, had just succeeded Francis Schmidt as TCU coach.

Meyer recognized immediately that in the gaunt, scrawny boy from Sweetwater he had a rare football jewel. Baugh had a slingshot arm. He could throw the ball like a bullet with the ease and accuracy of a man flipping a baseball. He also could nail a running target half the length of the field away.

Meyer spent hours working with Baugh. With Walter Roach as a swift, sure-fingered accomplice, they drilled on precision passing. They worked on hooks, comebacks, crossovers, posts and other maneuvers later popularized in professional football. It got so Baugh almost could hit a receiver with his eyes closed.

Baugh was an All-American selection in 1935 and 1936. During the 1936 season, Sammy completed 109 passes for 1,371 yards. He led TCU to a 9–6 triumph over a Santa Clara team that had gone into the final game as the only major unbeaten and untied team in the country. The Horned Frogs landed in the Cotton Bowl where Baugh led them to a 16–6 triumph over Marquette.

The ink was hardly dry on Baugh's passing records before a pint-sized understudy of the great Sammy, Davey O'Brien, came along to set new marks. Davey profited from the lessons given him by Baugh and from the assistance of an outstanding team that included such stars as All-American center Ki Aldrich and tackle I. B. Hale, who also played with Baugh.

Then came the magnificent teams of Texas A&M, powered by the churning legs of big John Kimbrough, and Texas, revived by Coach D. X. Bible and such aces as Pete Layden, Jack Crain, Roy Dale McKay and Joe Maglio. The Aggies put together a nineteen-game winning streak in 1939 and 1940. Texas won Conference championships in three of four years, starting with 1942.

From the early days of World War II to the present, the Southwest Conference has produced a steady stream of great football players and coaches, and the heroics that began in 1869 seem destined to continue as long as the game of football is fought.

In the following pages we hope to present the most dramatic games that the Southwest Conference has produced. It goes without saying that many will disagree with our selections, but controversy has never been lacking in football and we can only hope for your indulgence in what we feel to be the outstanding moment among many outstanding moments, wherein the heroes are legion.

1

The Game That Thrilled a Nation

NOVEMBER 30, 1935

SOUTHERN METHODIST   **20**

TEXAS CHRISTIAN   **14**

On November 30, 1935, sports enthusiasts in the United States woke up to the fact that a football game — a real football game — was being played in a place called Fort Worth, Texas. It was headlined as "Game of the Year." The National Broadcasting Company put it on the national network — the first such network broadcast to emanate from the Southwest. The top sportswriters were there dispensing the purple prose that marked the era. They included Grantland Rice, the man who picked the All-American teams; Bill Cunningham, the Boston phrasemaker; Joe Williams, the cryptic Scripps-Howard columnist; Maxwell Stiles from the West Coast, and several others.

Leading football coaches indulged in a busman's holiday for the occasion — Bernie Bierman from Minneapolis, Pappy Waldorf from Northwestern and Dana X. Bible, who was then coaching at Nebraska.

The game was a natural, pitting two unbeaten and untied powers — Texas Christian University and Southern Methodist University, both ranking at the top of the nation's unofficial ratings. Each had won ten games quite impressively. SMU had shut out seven of its foes and limited the other three to a single touchdown each. It had beaten a highly regarded UCLA team 21–0. Explosive TCU had averaged three touchdowns a game. The winner was sure to go to the Rose Bowl.

The individual aspects of the battle were even more intriguing. TCU had the rawboned Sammy Baugh, who could throw a football the way Dizzy Dean cut loose a baseball. He had a quick-wrist throw and the ball traveled with bullet velocity, so fast and sharp that receivers

*Slinging Sammy Baugh,
1934–35–36*

had a tough time holding it. A major league baseball prospect at short-stop, he had come to TCU on a baseball and basketball scholarship. He also was a tremendous kicker.

Aligned against him was a wisp of a little guy whom SMU partisans referred to lovingly as the Mighty Midget of Corsicana. His name was Bobby Wilson. He was only five feet, ten inches tall and weighed just 148 pounds, but he could spin on a dime and he was as elusive as a scared rabbit. His position was tailback in the traditional single-wing formation. But he lacked the triple-threat qualities usually demanded in that position. He couldn't punt and passing wasn't his game. But he could run — or rather scoot and wiggle. He was deadly on the buck lateral and he was an excellent pass receiver.

The rival coaches — Dutch Meyer of TCU and Matty Bell of SMU — were old friends but contrasts in techniques. Meyer was a small, stocky man who always wore a bowl haircut. He was given to inspirational pep talks and "Go get 'em" exhortations in the tradition of Notre Dame's Knute Rockne. They called him the Saturday Fox because of his repu-tation as a giant-killer. Bell was a tall, soft-spoken tactician with pierc-

*Matty Bell of SMU
and Dutch Meyer of TCU*

ing gray eyes. He was renowned as a defensive coach although his teams were always smart operators of the crisscross and multiple pass backfield maneuvers. They called him Moanin' Matty because of his usually pessimistic predictions.

But Bell was a moaner only when he felt it was to his psychological advantage. He could take the opposite tack when the impulse hit him, as he did astonishingly just before the big championship battle with TCU.

The game had been regarded as a standoff until it was found out that Harry Shuford, the SMU fullback and team leader who called the plays, had not been able to shake off a wrenched knee suffered in the UCLA game two weeks before and would be of little, if any, service.

"We're going to do the best we can," Bell told a group of writers and visiting coaches, "but without a man like Shufford, I'm afraid we don't have much chance."

Later, discussing the approaching game with a close newspaper friend, the SMU coach confided, "I think we'll win it."

Word got out, as Bell apparently hoped. Most of the observers, accustomed to Moanin' Matty, were stunned. Dutch Meyer, the TCU coach, was delighted. He had spent the week getting his Horned Frogs fired up for the occasion, and Bell's remark was just what he needed.

With Shuford out, TCU had to be favored. Besides Baugh, the Frogs had a fine halfback in Jimmy Lawrence, twice named on the Conference All-Star team. They had an All-America center in Darrell Lester and an All-Conference guard in Tracy Kellow.

SMU's Maurice Orr

SMU was strong on defense, as its record showed. The two tackles, Truman Spain and Maurice Orr, each towered six-five and weighed 215 pounds. J. C. (Iron Man) Wetsel was an All-America guard, a rough-tough operator. To step into Shuford's shoes, Bell brought up Bob Finley, a rather slight back, five-eleven and 185 pounds, whose principal duty had been punting.

During the week, it was noted that Bell spent a lot of time with Finley. After practice they would walk up and down the field, talking in low and mysterious tones. They mapped and remapped strategy. These small chats were to pay off later in the game.

It was interesting that Meyer and Bell approached the big battle from different psychological directions. Meyer had his TCU boys ready to jump out of their skins. On the field and in the locker rooms, he resorted to every inspirational device in the book. He wound up every workout with a rally and a speech that sent the athletes whooping and yelling to their dressing room.

By contrast, Bell played it cool with SMU, like a smart jockey rating his thoroughbred in the early stages of the race. "When I was at Texas A&M," he explained later, "we played Tulane's 1933 Rose Bowl team, and I never forgot the ice-water poise they had, the unexcited way they went about their business. I told myself if I ever had a great team I'd try to keep them in the same frame of mind."

Interest in the game was tremendous. Both Dallas, home of SMU, and Fort Worth, site of TCU, were decorated with signs and bunting which said, "On to the Rose Bowl." The TCU Stadium was a thirty-thousand sellout and you couldn't buy a pair of 40-yard-line tickets with a couple of oil wells.

At game time, the crush at the gates was so great that officials had to close them and get legitimate patrons into the stadium by hoisting them over the fence. This triggered the power of suggestion. Fans without tickets drove their cars to the edge of the fences and used them as springboards to jump over the barbed-wire barriers.

Such was the electric setting when the two teams arrived at the stadium by bus. The Horned Frogs of TCU, keyed to a high pitch, dashed onto the field, slapping each other's thighs and yelling, "Let's go, gang! Let's go! Let's get 'em, gang!" There was a moment of consternation when Coach Matty Bell, his assistants and the red-and-blue-clad SMU players walked out on the grass like men in a funeral procession.

If Bell had any doubts that his "cool it" psychology had reaped the proper results, these doubts were removed when he overheard Truman Spain talking to his fellow tackle, Maurice Orr. "Orr, you know what?" Spain said. "Those skunks think they're going to the Rose Bowl on our reputation."

As soon as the game began, it was obvious that Matty Bell had hit upon the better psychological strategy. SMU, cool and relaxed, moved to two early touchdowns for a 14–0 lead. TCU was too tight for an effective performance. Time after time, Baugh shot passes to receivers in the clear — Willie Walls and Walter Roach principally — but the ball skidded through their fingers. Sportswriter Grantland Rice, sitting in the press box, commented to his associates that Baugh was throwing too hard. "Why, he can knock a man down, throwing the ball like that," the white-haired Rice commented.

The SMU players also thought the fault lay with Baugh, who unleashed bullets. "I got my hand in front of one of them and it almost tore my finger off," said Bob Finley, who later was to spend seventeen years in professional baseball, part of the time with the Philadelphia Phillies.

Coach Meyer defended his passer. "It wasn't Baugh's fault," he said. "He threw the same way he did all year. The boys just weren't catching them. The passes were right in their hands but their fingers were stiff. They weren't relaxed. It was my fault for getting the team too high."

In all, nine of Baugh's passes were dropped. Roach alone dropped five. Walls and Jimmy Lawrence also let passes get away. "And they were the finest bunch of receivers I ever had," Meyer moaned.

SMU marched 73 yards for its first touchdown in the opening period. Sub fullback Finley called the signals and he did a superb job of it. Realizing that TCU defenses would be zeroing in on Wilson, the ball was given to the little All-America tailback only once during the drive. The Mustang drive featured reverses by wingback Shelley Burt and fake buck laterals that sent Finley smashing into the line. Finley scored from the one.

TCU may have been tense but it managed to snap back with a 74-yard drive of its own. The expedition might have resulted in a matching touchdown if the TCU receivers hadn't suddenly been stricken again with cold fingers. The drive stalled on the SMU 16.

Moments later, SMU struck again, this time going 80 yards on six plays. The featured strike was a 33-yard pass from Finley to Maco Stewart. Stewart caught the ball just as he went sprawling down on the nine-yard line. At this stage, SMU resorted to a bit of the old Aerial Circus. With the ball at the seven, Finley took the snap, handed off to Burt, who lateraled out to Wilson.

Nobody was more dumbfounded than the TCU defense. It was only the third time in the game that Wilson had handled the ball. He went across standing up, and SMU led 14–0. The experts were beginning to fidget. TCU had been made a firm six-point favorite and 7–2 in man-to-man betting.

The Horned Frogs were not without resources, not the least important of which was Sammy Baugh's booming right foot which later went on to set punting records in the National Football League. Baugh sent a spiraling punt 50 yards down the field and out-of-bounds on the SMU four. Backed against the wall, Finley tried to kick out of danger but he got off a bad kick which took a backward bounce and was downed on the 26.

The Frogs were a smartened, maddened lot at this stage. Fullback Tillie Manton and halfback Jimmy Lawrence shared smashes at the line that moved to the five. A pass interference call against SMU by Umpire Jack Mahan put the ball on the two. Lawrence scored and TCU went to the dressing room at half-time not completely in a state of rout. SMU led 14–7.

Coach Meyer needed little help in releasing the taut strings of his athletes' nerves. The fighting SMU team had done that, and it was a growling, unhappy, yet determined bunch of Horned Frogs who reviewed their first half sins and vowed amends during intermission.

A pleased Matty Bell stood before his SMU players and made only one comment. "You have thirty minutes to play," he said, "and a lifetime to think about it." It wasn't an original line, the SMU coach confessed afterward — he had picked it up from his coach in high school.

The third period was bitterly waged, but without score. Early in the fourth period, TCU started to give SMU something for its lifetime memory. Baugh completed a 14-yard pass to Lawrence. Then he hit

Jackrabbit Smith and Bobby Wilson of SMU doing chores before the Rose Bowl game

Lawrence again for 17 yards. This was indeed a different team than that which played the first half. The quick, tough Baugh faded back and — flick, flick, flick — he found his mark with rifle shots. A 17-yard pass to Walls, whose fingers now had become sure and relaxed, put the ball on the eight. Baugh spotted Lawrence in the end zone and almost knocked him down with a pass, but Lawrence reached and held on. The score now was tied 14–14.

It was a costly score for TCU, however. In twisting quickly to take the throw, Lawrence, the team's best runner, wrenched his knee. He was out of the game. There were thirteen minutes to play.

At this point, Coach Bell sent in a sub quarterback, a five-foot-nine, 165-pound scrambler named J. R. (Jackrabbit) Smith. It was a decision that was to have a vital effect on the outcome of the game. The little Jackrabbit got down to work immediately by returning the kickoff 27 yards to the SMU 47 — a spot which later pundits on television liked to refer to as "good field position." Smith was a feisty little scrapper who had a reputation of being very cocky. He shared signal-calling duties with Finley and now, having been inserted into the lineup in the final minutes, he had been given the job of running the team. He relished the challenge. He never looked over at the bench for instructions.

With Smith barking signals, SMU moved down to the TCU 37 and could go no farther. It was fourth down and four yards to go. Some ten minutes were left in the game. This was definitely a punt situation. Smith knew it. Smith knew that TCU knew it. Over on the SMU bench, a highly nervous Coach Matty Bell knew it — and expected it.

Jackrabbit snapped his team into the huddle. "Fake punt," he said. "Ends down and out. Pass to Wilson." The call surprised the Mustangs but there was no objection. Finley, the team's regular kicker, would be back in punt formation. He would throw the ball.

As the huddle broke up and the players bounced into position, Wilson passed close to Finley and counseled: "Listen, Bob, be sure to throw that ball as far as you can. I'll try to be out there. But make sure it gets to the end zone." Under the rules of the day, a pass incomplete in the end zone was a touchback, giving the rival team the ball on the 20-yard line.

Finley played his part well. If football players had been awarded Oscars for acting in those days, he would have been a certain winner. He took the snap from center, swung his leg as if to kick and then faded 10 yards back to throw. On the SMU bench, Coach Bell looked in disbelief and the blood slowly drained from his face. "What is he doing?" Bell exclaimed. Later he said, "I almost fainted."

Bobby Wilson on a 65-yard touchdown run against Texas A&M,
cementing an unbeaten, untied season for SMU

Wilson, operating from his flanker position, cut for the right sideline and headed down the field as fast as his bandy legs would carry
him. Finley backpedaled and, with the TCU rushers bearing down on
him, cut loose a prodigious heave. As soon as the ball left his hand,
he was smothered under a pile of purple-and-white jerseys.

It wasn't a wonderful pass, by technical analysis. "It was so high and
so long it looked like a dying dove hanging up there," Matty Bell
recalled later, with a shiver. "It was thrown on the wrong side of
Wilson," said Dutch Meyer.

Good, bad or indifferent, the pass and its gifted receiver got the
job done.

Those at the scene later gave differing accounts of how Wilson caught
the ball. Some contend he stopped, turned and came back to the ball.

Others say he snared it in full flight, reaching over his shoulder for it as he approached the 10-yard line. Dutch Meyer insists Wilson had to twist in midair and catch it over his right shoulder. Matty Bell said, "He fielded it like an outfielder." Kern Tips, longtime broadcaster of Southwest games and rated an outstanding authority, reported: "Wilson never swerved from a straight sideline path. On the TCU three-yard line he looked back, leaped high in the air, tipped down the football into control and hugged onto it as he scrambled into the TCU end zone, glad to be alive and part of passing a miracle."

The extra-point attempt was missed and SMU led 20–14, the score that held up until the end of the game.

With nine minutes to play, TCU still had a chance to pull the game out of the ashes but the tough Mustang defense refused to yield. Baugh's passing carried the Horned Frogs to the 28 and the 35 but they could go no farther. The TCU passer later was criticized for relying strictly on the air game in the final minutes when TCU had gained close to 200 yards on the ground.

Baugh had an explanation. "Without Lawrence, all I could do was throw," he said. It was a bitter blow for the favored Frogs, who felt confident they would have won the game except for Lawrence's injury. It was ironic that Wilson got behind Lawrence's substitute, Harold McClure, to make his dramatic catch.

Southern Methodist received the bid to the Rose Bowl in Pasadena, California, losing to Stanford, 7–0. "We outgained Stanford, but our boys never really bore down in that game," Bell said. TCU went to the Sugar Bowl and edged Louisiana State, 3–2.

Describing the SMU-TCU game, Grantland Rice wrote, "This was one of the greatest games ever played in the sixty-year history of the nation's finest college sport. In the most desperate game this season has known from coast to coast, Southern Methodist beat Texas Christian and thereby carved a clearcut highway right into the middle of the Rose Bowl beyond any argument . . . a swirl of action that no other section of the country could approach . . . the climax game of 1935."

Weeks after the game, Jackrabbit Smith, the audacious sub tailback who called the winning play, approached Matty Bell and said: "Coach, I've been thinking about that fourth-down play. If TCU had got the ball and won the game, they'd have run me out of town."

"Yeah," said Bell, "and they'd have run me out right with you."

Davey O'Brien of TCU

2
Davey O'Brien: One Hundred Fifty Pounds of TNT

SUGAR BOWL: JANUARY 2, 1939

TEXAS CHRISTIAN 15
CARNEGIE TECH   7

If the reeling opponents of Texas Christian felt a wave of relief when Sammy Baugh and his slingshot arm came to the end of the varsity string in 1937, they were in for a rude jolt and disappointment. With Baugh's departure, Coach Dutch Meyer was now ready to pull the fuse on his new secret weapon — 150 pounds of TNT named Davey O'Brien. If Baugh, with his pinpoint passing, gave Southwest Conference teams nightmares, it remained for O'Brien to turn them into candidates for a psychiatrist's couch and the straitjacket.

"Baugh might have been a better all-around player than Davey, and a better passer," Meyer said, "but as a field general O'Brien has never been equaled. He was the finest play selector I have ever seen."

O'Brien understudied the great Baugh in 1936 and blossomed in 1937 but did not reach full flower until 1938 when he led the Horned Frogs through a perfect 10–0 season and then became the master architect of TCU's 15–7 triumph over Carnegie Tech in the Sugar Bowl. They called it O'Brien's greatest game — fitting climax to an historic varsity career.

O'Brien was just a twig of a man. As a youngster with an enthusiasm for football, he was chided by his friends because of frail physique. When he said he wanted to go to TCU, his teammates laughed.

"We told Davey he was ridiculous and ought to forget it," said Allie White, who played tackle on O'Brien's teams at TCU. "We were wrong. I doubt if there will ever be another his equal."

Dutch Meyer called the 1938 TCU team "the finest college football team I have ever seen."

Ki Aldrich, TCU's outstanding lineman

Besides O'Brien at quarterback, the Horned Frogs had two other All-America players — Ki Aldrich at center and linebacker, and I. B. Hale at tackle. "Ki was the best man I've ever seen at sizing up plays," Meyer said. "He was a football birddog. The line was big and strong.

The backfield was versatile. Every man could run, block and catch passes."

The TCU forward wall was a senior line averaging 208 pounds. Don Looney and Durward Horner were at ends. Hale and Allie White were at tackles, Forrest Kline and Bud Taylor were at guards and Aldrich at center. Kline weighed 248 pounds, Hale 244, Aldrich 215. Taylor, at 195, was the only member of the line under 200.

TCU opened the 1938 season by beating Centenary, 13–0, and followed with a 21–14 triumph over Arkansas. Then the Horned Frogs proceeded to grind past other opponents like some huge earthmoving piece of machinery, never trailing in a game and winning most of them by one-sided margins.

The major regular season test came on November 26 against Southern Methodist, which had lost bouts with Marquette and Pittsburgh but which had won all its Conference games and thus had come up to TCU in the finale with the title at stake.

The game was played in swirling winds. Because of the conditions, O'Brien, the master tactician, chose his plays well. He rarely passed. Only one pass was used among the fourteen plays in the first TCU touchdown drive in the opening quarter. The Frogs marched on the ground 39 yards for another score after a scooting, squirming punt return by O'Brien. The tiny TCU quarterback caught SMU napping and scored a third touchdown on a 37-yard pass. Southern Methodist managed to block a kick in the fourth quarter which led to its lone score, TCU winning 20–7.

At that time, the Southwest Conference had no binding commitment with the Cotton Bowl. The Texas Christian players were polled. They

TCU's first team in a practice charge

voted to go to the Sugar Bowl in New Orleans. Their opponent was Carnegie Tech, the strongest team in the East and, at the time, one of the most publicized. Carnegie Tech had been the victim of one of the most monumental goofs in college football history and this had resulted in the team's only defeat during the season.

It happened October 22, 1938, in South Bend, Indiana, in the game against Notre Dame. In the fourth quarter of the scoreless game, Carnegie Tech had the ball in midfield. The quarterback asked Referee John Getchell the number of the down. "Third down," Getchell said.

Carnegie Tech tried a run and failed to make first down. Then as the team was going into a huddle for what it thought was fourth down, Getchell rushed over and said he had made a mistake. Carnegie Tech had used up its downs, he said, and the ball must be turned over to Notre Dame. Bill Kern, the Carnegie Tech coach, protested vehemently. The Carnegie Tech players stormed around the referee, arguing wildly. Getchell stuck to his guns. Notre Dame took over and pressed to the only touchdown of the game, winning 7–0.

Despite the furore, Carnegie Tech showed a rare faculty for forgiveness by selecting "Wrong Down" Getchell to officiate in the Sugar Bowl game. Getchell later apologized for his error but added, "It was a lucky error. It allowed me to see the greatest football game I ever saw."

Fifty thousand fans turned out at the Sugar Bowl January 2, 1939, for the match between two unusual teams. All eyes were on O'Brien, the phenomenal little passing genius who had become the first player to win all three of college football's major trophies — the Heisman, Maxwell and Camp awards — as the outstanding individual player of the year.

The two teams fenced cagily through the opening minutes but late in the first quarter Texas Christian gained possession at midfield — actually it was Carnegie Tech's 48 — and O'Brien marched his team systematically to the game's first touchdown. The wee signal-caller mixed his passes and ground plays smartly in moving down to the Tartans' six-yard line. Aldrich opened a gaping hole at center and fullback Connie Sparks drove across the goal. O'Brien, normally an accurate place-kicker, missed the try for point but TCU had drawn first blood, 6–0.

The game produced a succession of fast-breaking climaxes but it was not until the final minute of the second period that Carnegie Tech was able to match TCU's touchdown. Pete Moroz, a lightweight back not much larger than O'Brien, threw a long, arching pass from the Frogs' 44. George Muha made a leaping catch on the one-yard line

*O'Brien, harnessed by Arkansas, is still able to get
the ball away*

and fell across for the score. Muha then kicked the extra point, giving
Carnegie Tech a 7–6 lead at the half. It marked the first time during
the season that Texas Christian had fallen behind in a game.

Texas Christian lost no time asserting its supremacy in the second
half. While the huge TCU line threw back every Carnegie Tech threat,
O'Brien got his team rolling. In the third period, Davey led the Horned
Frogs 80 yards on five plays for the go-ahead touchdown. Two long
passes accounted for most of the yardage. The first was a 35-yard pass
from O'Brien to Earl Clark. The second was a 44-yarder to Durwood
Horner, who caught the ball at the 30 and ran the remainder of the
way for the score. The try for point again failed and TCU's lead was
an uncomfortable 12–7.

Later in the period, Bill Condit, Carnegie Tech halfback, broke loose
and appeared headed for a sure touchdown. After covering 17 yards,
there was only one man left between him and the goal line. That was
Davey O'Brien. O'Brien made a leaping tackle and brought Condit
thudding to earth at the TCU 26. Moments later, the threat died when
big Ki Aldrich intercepted a fourth-down pass.

Early in the fourth period, O'Briend launched another drive that carried to the Carnegie Tech one. The Tartans rose up in a body and held. On fourth down, O'Brien, undaunted by his previous failures to convert the extra point, dropped back and kicked a 20-yard field goal that put the game momentarily out of danger.

With Aldrich and his mates throwing up a wall of pig-iron, the lead held and the game went to Texas Christian, 15–7.

O'Brien, in addition to directing an almost flawless attack, hit on 17 of 28 passes for 225 yards. He and his teammates netted 142 yards on the ground while Carnegie Tech was held to 59 in the air and 129 on the ground.

After the game, a Carnegie Tech player was asked why the Tartans' big linemen didn't make an effort to punish the tiny O'Brien and get him out of the game.

"We'd rather lose than to have won that way," the player replied. "After all, we do not feel a bit disgraced, losing to a great little guy like that."

The game rang down the curtain on a fabulous career for the under-sized giant of TCU football. O'Brien gained 2,834 yards during his career — passing, running, returning punts and interceptions. He was responsible for 229 points. He set a Conference record for pass completions with 110, one more than Baugh, which gained 1,733 yards, also a record at the time.

"O'Brien was a back of multiple talents with a heart and head for football," wrote Fred Russell and George Leonard in *Big Bowl Football*. "Only once in his career did he require a time-out. He was fearless, never flinching when rushed by merciless giant linemen. He had complete confidence in his ability to pass accurately and would fire unhesitatingly if his target had no more than a one-step lead."

The Associated Press said, "O'Brien has no peer in collegiate football today. In six straight victories, he threw 103 passes and 54 were completed for 1,018 yards. Add ruggedness, signal-calling ability, kicking and brilliant running to the little fellow's makeup and you've got TCU's leader."

When O'Brien closed his collegiate career, Texas Christian retired and enshrined his "No. 8" jersey.

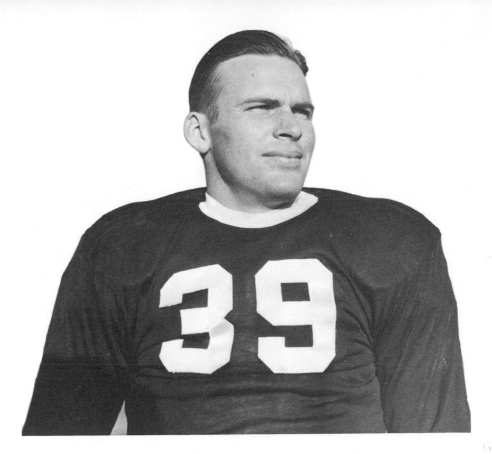

3

Jarrin' John Kimbrough: The Runaway Truck

NOVEMBER 9, 1940

TEXAS A & M	19
SOUTHERN METHODIST	7

After Sammy Baugh and Davey O'Brien had run their spectacular course at Texas Christian, football fans of the Southwest were hit with the shocking and unnerving discovery that the football sometimes could be moved as effectively on the ground as through the air.

The man responsible for this revelation was fullback John Kimbrough of Texas A&M, a powerful hulk of a man who ran with the devastation of a berserk concrete mixer. He was an All-America selection in 1939 and 1940 during which time the Aggies won eighteen games and lost only one. The Aggies won the Southwest Conference

Kimbrough, Coach Homer Norton, and Joe Routt

championship with a 10–0 record in 1939 and shared it with Southern Methodist with an 8–1 mark in 1940.

"Jarrin' Jawn" Kimbrough — as Texans reverently referred to him — stood six-three in the air and weighed 220 pounds. Despite his size, he ran the hundred yards in close to ten seconds flat. He ran with high knee action and was dangerous both straightaway and to the outside.

In picking his all-time college backfield, Homer Norton, coach of the Aggies, put Kimbrough in the quartet with Red Grange, Jim Thorpe and Bronko Nagurski. "He could run the ends as well as he could crash through the line," Norton said. "He had big legs, an inextinguishable will to win and he was never down until they had every inch of him on the ground."

During his varsity career, Kimbrough played innumerable outstanding games. He provided the punch to a team that fought its way to the national championship and barely missed a trip to the Rose Bowl after playing in the Sugar Bowl in 1940.

Some writers point to the Sugar Bowl game of 1940 — with seventy-three thousands fans packed on newly-poured concrete — as the high mark in Big John's series of Herculean performances. The majority vote, however, goes to the game with Southern Methodist at Dallas on November 9, 1940.

Kimbrough with ball following James Thomason

In that 1940 Sugar Bowl game, Texas A&M, unbeaten, untied and ranked No. 1 nationally, took on a powerful Tulane team that had swept to the Southeastern Conference title. Kimbrough was one of four Aggie players who went the full sixty minutes without relief, playing both offense and defense. The others were halfback Jim Thomason, guard Marshall Foch Robnett and end Herb Smith.

With Kimbrough hammering out yardage in small, vicious hunks, the Aggies moved to Tulane's one-yard line in the first quarter only to be stopped dead by the Greenies' swarming defense. Later, the Aggies got the ball on Tulane's 32 after a short punt and went to a score, Kimbrough plunging over from the one.

There was no score in the second period but in the third, Tulane's fleet Bobby Kellogg raced 75 yards for the touchdown that tied the score 7–7. Then Tulane took advantage of a fumble on the A&M 39 and scored early in the last period for a 13–7 lead. Herbie Smith broke through to block Johnny Thibaut's try for the extra point — a vital play.

The Aggies, smarting, called upon their giant ballcarrier and went to work with a vengeance. Big John rammed the center and swept the ends. On one play he slashed 18 yards. The drive carried 70 yards.

Kimbrough scored the decisive touchdown. With the ball on Tulane's 18-yard line late in the game, Walemon Price tossed an eight-yard over-the-line pass to Herbie Smith. Smith, seeing himself trapped by a wall of Tulane green jerseys, flipped a lateral to Kimbrough. Smith took out the defensive left halfback. Kimbrough shook off two tacklers and rambled the final 10 yards. Price kicked the extra point that gave the game to the Aggies, 14–13.

Kimbrough carried the ball twenty-six times. He rolled up 152 yards.

"I never thought I'd have the honor of tackling a truck," Tulane's Buddy Banker said afterwards, "but that's just what it was like to hit Kimbrough."

From this Sugar Bowl victory, the Aggies moved into the 1940 campaign with a team which Coach Norton described as equally as good as his national champion eleven of 1939 but one beset by overconfidence. "They played like pros," the A&M coach said. "At times, they were too sure of themselves."

Nevertheless, the mighty Aggies, with Kimbrough shattering defensive lines, continued to bowl over opponent after opponent. They crushed Texas A&I and Tulsa. They squeezed by UCLA, then beat Texas Christian, Baylor and Arkansas, piling up 126 points while yielding only 20 to their first six foes.

They were working on a seventeen-game winning streak when they came against Southern Methodist at Dallas. SMU hadn't been idle. The explosive Mustangs, with a dangerous passer in Ray Mallouf, had beaten UCLA, North Texas State, and Auburn and Texas, and had tied Pittsburgh. Nobody doubted that this was the game to decide the Conference championship.

November 9, 1940, was a rainy, miserable day in Dallas. It was no weather for man or beast — nor for Mallouf's passing, nor for Kimbrough's running. The two teams sparred cautiously, waiting for the first break. It came suddenly in the midst of a punting duel between the Aggies' Bill Conatser and SMU's Presto Johnston. Conatser sent a 60-yard boot into the coffin corner — on SMU's one-yard line. Johnston kicked back only 32 yards.

Now the Aggies were in good field position for the first time. It was at this point that Coach Homer Norton, knowing that the Mustangs were ready to key on Kimbrough, did some shuffling in his attack. He transformed blocking back Jim Thomason into a ballcarrier. He moved Kimbrough from fullback to tailback from which position he could run, pass or kick. The maneuver rattled SMU. The Aggies scored in four plays. First came a 17-yard pass. Then a nine-yard run by Thomason, four by Kimbrough and a three-yard touchdown plunge by Conatser. The extra point made it 7–0.

"Kimbrough was a terrific weapon just by being in there," Norton said later. "They kept expecting us to throw our right — we hit them with everything else."

The Mustangs hit back in the second period by filling the air with footballs. Although the turf was slippery and the football was like a greased watermelon, SMU sustained a drive and went to a matching touchdown. The score came on a 33-yard pass by Mallouf into the end zone. An Aggie defender batted it, but Bobby Brown grabbed it before it touched the ground. Johnston kicked the extra point and the score was tied 7–7.

The Dallas stands were wild with excitement. The Mustangs had stopped the great John Kimbrough and they had a good chance for victory. But they were doomed to disappointment. Kimbrough, they discovered, simply had not taken the wraps off his churning legs.

In the third period, Conatser took a Johnston punt on his own 25 and ran it back through a broken field to the SMU 35. It was here that Coach Norton sent in terse instructions, "Give it to John."

Kimbrough smashed at the middle. Kimbrough tore off tackle. Kimbrough circled the ends. A&M needed nine plays to go the 35 yards and Big John carried on seven of them, finally scoring from the two.

"It was one of the greatest shows of pile-driving football that the Southwest had seen," wrote one observer, J. W. Williams.

The extra point attempt failed, however, and A&M's lead was 13–7. It was too close for comfort, particularly with SMU's Ray Mallouf all fired up and ready to hit back.

Late in the third period, Mallouf started hitting on his passes and moved his team to the Aggies' 24. Then he cut loose with an arching pass intended to go all the way. Kimbrough threw his huge frame in front of the ball and intercepted it at his own 10. The defensive feat saved a touchdown that might have put SMU ahead.

In the fourth period, Thomason, playing brilliantly on defense as well as offense, blocked an SMU punt on the edge of the Mustang goal line. Jim Sterling and Joe Routt both pounced on the ball in the end zone to give the Aggies another score. The game ended Texas A&M 19, Southern Methodist 7. It was the eighteenth straight triumph for the Aggies.

The Aggies made it the nineteenth by shellacking Rice 25–0 and went against Texas in the final game of the season, heavily favored and with a sure Rose Bowl bid hinging on a victory.

It was then that A&M's overconfidence — recognized by Coach Norton — proved the team's undoing. The Aggies were flat. Even with the great Kimbrough, they could make no inroads in Texas' quick, agile line. A&M kicked off to the Longhorns and Texas had a score on the board before the Aggies had another chance to feel the football.

Pete Layden, Texas' quarterback, hit on two passes — one to Jack Crain to move the ball from the Texas 34 to the Aggie 33 and another to Noble Doss, who tumbled out-of-bounds on the one-yard line. Layden dove across for the touchdown and Crain kicked the extra point. As it developed, the entire game was crammed into those first fifty-seven seconds.

The Aggies, proud national champions, hammered away at the Texas line, moving the ball well between the 20-yard stripes but finding no daylight when in enemy territory. Texas was too busy trying to stop Jarrin' Jawn Kimbrough to muster much of an attack of its own.

So the game ended: Texas 7, A&M 0. Also ended was the Aggies' nineteen-game winning streak. The Rose Bowl trip was out. The Aggies had to settle for a tie with SMU for the Conference championship.

But, thanks to John Kimbrough, they had had their day. And now the Southwest could breathe easy again. There was such a thing as the forward pass.

4
The Day That Bobby Scored Them All

COTTON BOWL: JANUARY 1, 1946

TEXAS	40
MISSOURI	27

A couple of years ago sportswriters of the Southwest Conference were called upon to vote for the greatest football players to perform in the league over the last twenty years, or since World War II — an All-Era Eleven, so to speak.

The No. 1 choice was Doak Walker, brilliant backfield star at Southern Methodist University in 1945–49. Chosen in the same backfield, close to Walker in the voting, was Bobby Layne, who quarterbacked the rampaging Texas teams in 1944–47. Layne and Walker were teammates on the Highland Park High School team in Dallas — Layne a year ahead. They were the closest of friends who held each other in the highest respect and admiration. They went into the U. S. Merchant Marine together and came out at the same time. Only a quirk of fate kept them from playing on the same college team.

Bobby helped lead Highland Park to the bi-district title in 1942 and to the state high school semifinals in 1943. Upon graduation, he moved in with an uncle, a strong supporter of the Texas Longhorns, and played freshman varsity with Texas in 1944, while wartime restrictions against

Blair Cherry, Longhorn coach

freshman play were waived. Walker, with another year at Highland Park, meanwhile led his team to the state high school finals.

When Doak was graduated from high school in 1945, the war was still in progress. He and his pal, Bobby, joined the U. S. Merchant Marine. The war suddenly took a quick and favorable turn, and their service was brief. On the last Saturday in October, 1945, Bobby and Doak reported to New Orleans to receive their discharges from the service. It was a coincidence that their longtime friend and former coach at Highland Park High, H. N. (Rusty) Russell, also was in New Orleans on another mission. Rusty had moved in as assistant coach at Southern Methodist and the Mustangs were in the Crescent City for a game with Tulane. There was a happy reunion.

Also in New Orleans at the time was Blair Cherry, assistant to Coach D. X. Bible at Texas. Cherry was scouting SMU for the next week's game against his Longhorns. He was happy to see Layne but happier to see Layne's young friend and ex-teammate, Walker, widely sought by all Southwest Conference schools.

"Maybe we can get that boy to come to Texas," Cherry confided to Layne.

"Perhaps," said Layne, hopefully.

Doak was not committed but was leaning heavily toward his old high school coach, Rusty Russell, and his hometown university, SMU. Russell knew he couldn't dissuade Layne from returning to Texas but he hoped to keep Bobby from influencing the Doaker, and, somewhat ambivalently, he gave the two boys tickets to the SMU–Tulane game.

It was almost a fatal blunder. SMU played miserably, losing to Tulane 19–7. After the game, Layne said to Doak, "You better come to Texas with me. Let's go over and talk to Coach Cherry."

"Okay," Walker said, his mind not fully made up.

The two young men raced to Cherry's hotel. The story is that, as they were going up the elevator to the coach's room, Cherry was coming down another lift to check out. They missed each other completely.

Walker returned to Dallas and immediately enrolled at SMU. Layne returned to Texas. So the two buddies took separate roads and, instead of winding up in the same backfield, they became opponents. Within a week they were aligned on opposite sides of the field, launching one of the Southwest's most exciting and colorful personal rivalries.

Walker, who never had played a minute of college football, said afterward that he didn't know how he made such a quick transition. "Bobby and I got out of the service on Friday," he recalled. "On the following Monday, both of us were in uniform, practicing. The next Saturday we were playing against each other — I as a freshman, Bobby as a sophomore."

The first meeting of these two former teammates was dramatic. Walker ran 32 yards for a touchdown that put SMU ahead 7–0. Layne rallied Texas in the final period. Bobby passed to Dale Schwartzkopf for one touchdown and, after intercepting a Walker pass, threw to R. E. (Pappy) Blount for a 12–7 Texas victory.

With the impetus of this triumph, the Longhorns went on to whip Baylor, Texas Christian and Texas A&M for a 5–1–0 Conference record and a bid to the Cotton Bowl. They were arrayed against the Missouri Tigers, champions of the Big Six, and the result was the greatest football day in the life of Robert Lawrence Layne. It was the most spectacular point-making orgy in the history of the Cotton Bowl. Texas won 40–27, erasing the previous high-scoring mark — Alabama's 29–21 victory over Texas A&M in 1942.

In addition to the 67 points, the game produced a total of 980 yards gained. Texas had touchdown marches of 80, 75, 74, 69, 60 and 60 yards. Missouri had scoring expeditions of 93, 80, 80 and 62 yards. Missouri ran up 22 first downs, Texas 19.

Missouri, with a 285-pound tackle named Jim Kekeris and a 139-

pound quarterback named Leonard Brown, outgained the Texans, 514 yards to 466 yards, but it was strictly Bobby Layne's day. The Texas quarterback figured in every point put on the Longhorns' side of the scoreboard. He ran for three touchdowns, he threw for two and caught a long pass himself for a sixth. He kicked four extra points. His passing exhibition was phenomenal. He completed 11 of 12 throws. Altogether, Texas hit on nine passes in a row and, after the 10th was broken up, connected on four more to make the day's harvest 13 out of 14.

"I'm sure I would have to call it my biggest day in football," Layne, who went on to quarterback the Detroit Lions to two championships in the pro National Football League, recalled later. "I remember it was a wild game. Neither team had much of a defense. It seemed every time one got the ball, it went for a touchdown. There must not have been more than a couple of punts all day."

Porous defenses or no, the game provided a thrilling, non-stop spectacle for the 45,507 spectators who gathered in Dallas' Cotton Bowl that clear, crisp Tuesday afternoon, January 1, 1946.

Texas, with a 9–1 record overall, ruled a 14-point favorite. The Missouri Tigers had got off to a late start. They were beaten by Minnesota 34–0. They lost to Ohio State 47–6 and they suffered a 14–7 setback at the hands of Michigan State, all games against tough Big Ten rivals. Yet they rallied to win their own title in the Big Six.

The Longhorns realized, nevertheless, that they were up against a formidable foe. Kekeris, at tackle, was a mountain of a man and the rest of the line was big and menacing, outweighing the lighter but quicker Texas forward wall by perhaps twenty pounds to the man. Missouri's leading scorer, Lloyd Brinkman, was ailing. But quarterback Leonard Brown, nicknamed Mickey Mouse, was a veritable bombshell.

Jim Kekeris, Missouri's fearsome lineman who gave Texas pause for thought

Lennie Brown, Missouri's great back who bedeviled Texas in a losing cause

From the moment that big Harlan Wetz put his toe to the ball on the Texas kickoff an offensive game seemed to be in the offing. The ball sailed over the goal line for a touchback and Missouri took it on the 20 and proceeded to march past midfield before being forced to punt — the only punt of the first half. Layne took the punt at the 20 and returned it to his own 25. Then he drove the Texas team 75 yards to the opening touchdown. He alternated with Ralph Ellsworth and Joe Baumgardner in moving the ball on the ground to the Missouri 48. Then he switched to the air. From the 48, he sailed a long pass to Baumgardner, who caught the ball on the 13 and ran the rest of the way. Layne kicked the extra point.

Missouri took the ensuing kickoff and scored the matching touchdown in four plays, the last a 65-yard pass from quarterback Bill Dellastatious to end Roland Oakes. Two runs by Dellastatious and one by Brinckman covered 15 yards to the Missouri 35. Then Dellastatious stepped back and cut loose a high, wobbly pass, which Oakes gathered in on the Texas 40 and outlegged the Longhorn secondary for the score. Kekeris kicked the extra point, and the score was 7–7.

The Longhorns' Jack Halfpenny received the next kickoff but fumbled at the Texas 40, Wetz fortunately recovering to regain possession. It took ten plays for Texas to cover the 60 remaining yards, most of it on the ground. Baumgardner had a 23-yard sprint in the march and Layne one of 16. Layne slammed over from the one on a keeper play and kicked the point. Score: Texas 14, Missouri 7.

Before the first period ended, Missouri had launched another drive which, with a couple of interruptions and quick ball changes, resulted in a tying touchdown early in the second period. The Tigers took the kickoff, smashed 55 yards to the Texas 25 before bogging down. Kekeris's field goal attempt went wide. Texas proceeded to pound back to the Missouri 38 — on a smashing running game — only to lose the ball when Bill Gillory, a sub halfback, fumbled a handoff from Layne. Bob Clodfelter recovered for Missouri on the Tiger 38 and then the Tigers went all the way — 62 yards in eight plays. The diminutive, squirming Brown was the spearhead of this drive, spinning 19 yards on one play and grabbing a batted ball on another. Layne came close to halting the march when he got his hands on a Dellastatious pass but he batted the ball into Brown's hands and Missouri kept its drive alive. The Tigers moved to the Texas three and then, with giant Kekeris single-handedly moving the whole right side of the Texas line, Dellastatious knifed across for the score. Kekeris kicked the point and the score was a level 14–14.

Now it was Texas' time to have fun in this weird game of give and take. From the kickoff, their strike-back covered 69 yards, 56 of the distance gained on a tricky lateral-forward maneuver. Layne lateraled to Jack Jackson, a sub halfback, who threw to end Hubert Bechtol, tackled on the 13 by Dellastatious. Another pass, Layne to Bechtol, and two short runs shoved the ball to the one, where Layne ran it over. Layne again kicked the point.

This made the score at the half: Texas 21, Missouri 14. The Cotton Bowl crowd was limp from excitement when it went to the refreshment stands. The second half, they said to each other, couldn't possibly be as thrilling. But it was.

The Longhorns pounced on a quick break early in the third period and enlarged their lead. Shortly after the kickoff, Missouri's Bob Hopkins fumbled and guard David Green recovered for Texas on the Missouri 20. Layne rifled a short pass to Bechtol for five yards and hit Baumgardner from the 15 for the touchdown. Layne proved he was human — he missed the try for the extra point.

Although it was Baumgardner who caught two of Layne's touchdown passes, Bechtol proved the favorite target for the sharpshooting Texas quarterback. Bechtol made eight catches.

There was only one score in the third period, but this was a merciful respite for the goggle-eyed spectators who were to see no less than four touchdowns — two on each side — in the wild final quarter. The third period score came on a 15-yard pass, Layne to Baumgardner, after Bob Hopkins had recovered a fumble on the Missouri 20.

Missouri scored first in the last period, climaxing a 93-yard surge

Hub Bechtol of Texas

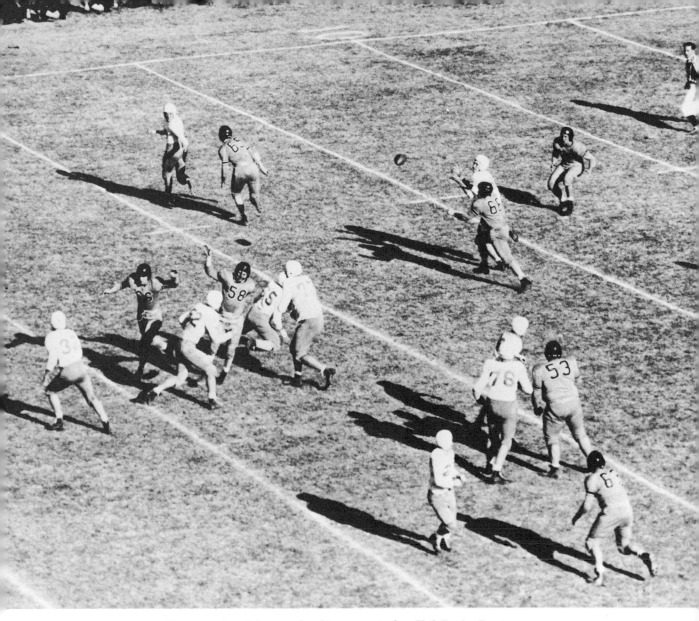

Layne, at far right, watches his pass spiral to Hub Bechtol's arms

that started in the final minutes of the preceding quarter. The Texas captain, Jim Plyler, who had been suffering from an attack of influenza, had entered the game for the first time and put the Tigers deep in the hole by punting the ball dead on the Tiger seven. Brown and Bob Hopkins played featured roles in the uninterrupted foray which covered almost the length of the field. Brown was a squirming, ducking, dodging dervish that kept the Longhorn defenders in a near state of panic every time Missouri had the ball. Hopkins ran with speed and power. In this early Missouri drive, Hopkins took a lateral from Brown, turned Bechtol's end and scampered 31 yards on one play. Howard Bonnett broke through a gaping hole made by Kekeris and scampered 21 yards for the touchdown.

Texas took the kickoff and rolled 81 yards to a score of its own. Layne completed passes to Bechtol and Ellsworth to bring the ball to midfield. Then he turned receiver. Catching the Missouri team completely off guard, Ellsworth went into passing position while Layne raced downfield. Layne caught the ball over his shoulder at the 15 — a 35-yard pass — and ran the remaining distance for the fifth touchdown in which he had a part. The Longhorns tried to convert on a pass from Billy Andrews to Layne but Andrews overshot his mark.

"Now it's our turn," said the Tigers as they took the kickoff on their 20. By this time it appeared that the defense lineups of both teams were on the field simply as props. Both sides moved the ball at will.

Missouri's final touchdown drive was relentless, and little Leonard Brown was superb. Brown turned left end for 42 yards. Three Missouri blockers were ahead of him and they mowed down Texas would-be tacklers as a minesweeper would. Brown and Hopkins ripped the Texas line to shreds and finally Hopkins went across from the one as a climax to the 80-yard drive.

This made the score 33–27 in favor of Texas, but the Longhorns had a little time left — enough to go 60 yards just to make the victory conclusive. Layne passed to Bechtol for 10 and then connected with his favorite receiver for 21. Texas moved to the Missouri four. Ellsworth picked up two. Then he tried again. This time, trapped, Ellsworth lateraled to Layne, who slashed the final two yards for a touchdown — the sixth of the day which carried his imprint. Going back in an attempt to kick the extra point, he knew he mustn't miss, even though his teammates didn't need it. The ball split the uprights.

Texas had won it, 40–27. Cotton Bowl fans had been treated to the maddest, highest-scoring game ever played in the Dallas oval. And Layne had his greatest collegiate day.

But the wild contest paid additional dividends. Leonard Brown, the 139-pound Missouri quarterback, was a vial of TNT. He called his own signal 18 times and ran for 121 yards, a rushing performance surpassed only by that of teammate Bob Hopkins, 16 carries for 125 yards. Little Lenny threw passes. He caught passes. He slammed vicious blocks against men almost twice his size. Time and time again he wrapped himself around the legs of Texas ballcarriers when he was the lone obstacle between the runner and the goal. Kekeris gave an All-America performance of brute strength.

It was such a wide-open offensive battle that Missouri gave up the ball on downs only twice, lost it once on a fumble and once on a pass interception. The Tigers punted twice. Texas scored every time it got its hands on the ball except when it fumbled once in the second and had to punt twice in the third.

"It was a thrilling game — the outcome was in doubt all the way," said Dana X. Bible, the veteran Texas coach. Bible delighted Texas fans by throwing in Billy (Rooster) Andrews, a football student manager who was only five feet five inches tall and weighed 135 pounds. Rooster wore jersey number 99. He carried water buckets for the team, practiced and suffered with it, occasionally kicked extra points and won a letter. His personal claim to fame: he was a roommate of the great Bobby Layne.

"Layne is simply marvelous," said Missouri's coach, Chauncey Simpson. "I never saw a better job by anybody on a football field."

Layne, a six foot one inch, 190-pound fiery competitor, went on to lead Texas through two more successful seasons, earning All-America honors in 1947, and then enjoying an illustrious pro career. In 1946, Texas opened with Missouri, winning this time 42–0, and closed with an 8–2 season. In 1947, Texas had a 9–1 record but lost the Conference title to Southern Methodist, which wound up 9–0–1. Doak Walker outdueled his old teammate in their final game as rivals, 14–13.

"Bobby never really lost a football game," the Doaker once said afterward. "Time just ran out on him."

Layne was the first great T formation quarterback in the Southwest Conference.

"His passing form wasn't classic, nor was he a clever runner," said his coach, Blair Cherry, who later succeeded Bible. "But Bobby was a winner."

One of the greatest backfields in football history: Doak Walker, Paul Page,
Dick McKissick, and Kyle Rote of SMU, as photographed in 1948

5

The Day Doak Missed

NOVEMBER 29, 1947

SOUTHERN METHODIST	**19**
TEXAS CHRISTIAN	**19**

The big clock in the end zone at TCU Stadium was whirring toward the "0" mark when Gil Johnson shot a pass to Sid Halliday over the goal line. The ball hit Halliday's stomach like the thump of a catcher's mitt, and the Southern Methodist end hugged it as he would a long-lost friend and crumbled to the ground.

Touchdown, SMU!

In the broadcast booth high above the stadium, Bill Stern, describing the game for a national radio audience, was caught up in the hysteria that swept thirty-two thousand fans. "SMU goes ahead, 19 to 19!" Stern screamed into the mike, befuddling millions.

It was quite true that the score was 19–19, but the game wasn't over. Fifteen seconds were left on the clock. Southern Methodist had a try for the extra point, which, if made, obviously would win it. There wasn't a single one among the thirty-two thousand — the howling, leaping SMU supporters and the dejected followers of the Horned Frogs — who wasn't convinced that the decisive point would be made. Going back into the kicking position was Ewell Doak Walker, Jr., who had become a legendary football figure at SMU. Walker — runner, passer, blocker, kicker — had successfully place-kicked 18 extra points during the season. He was a player who came up to the big moment.

Begrimed, weary, his chest heaving heavily, Doak walked back to the kicking position. The whole stadium was tense. Gil Johnson was down on his knees to hold the ball. The center snap was perfect. Johnson's grab and placement were quick. Walker's right leg whipped through the motion and the ball sailed toward the goalposts but veered wide to the left.

The kick failed. Final score: SMU 19, TCU 19.

Pandemonium broke loose. Southern Methodist players rushed out to where the dejected Walker stood and hoisted him to their shoulders. By the hundreds, fans poured onto the field, yelling, "Doak! Doak! He's the greatest!"

It was an ironic climax to what many believe to be the finest individual one-day performance ever executed in the career of Doak Walker, a 12-letter athlete at Highland Park High School, three-time All-American at Southern Methodist, Heisman Trophy winner, later star halfback and captain of the Detroit Lions in the professional National Football League.

Walker was born to greatness and was headed for football immortality almost from the day he was big enough to walk. When he was three days old, friends slapped his father on his back and jested, "Well, Ewell, what's he going to be when he grows up — President?"

"He's going to be an All-American," the elder Walker, a teacher and a football coach, replied solemnly. The friends laughed heartily. "A great kidder, that Ewell," they said.

The father, a center and tackle at Austin College in Sherman, Texas, gave young Doak a football helmet when the boy was two years old. He fed him shovel passes, taught him to throw, to relax his wrists, to block and tackle. He showed the boy how to run with his knees high, how to feint, duck and dart. He spent hours teaching the youngster punting, drop-kicking and place-kicking.

Walker was never an imposing athlete, and coaches appeared at a loss to put a finger on the attribute or attributes which made him great. He stood five feet eleven inches tall and weighed 165 pounds. He was square-shouldered and bullnecked. He lacked the lean, racehorse qualities of a thoroughbred back. Yet no one ever questioned his thoroughbred qualities. He wasn't particularly fast. He once was clocked in 10.2 seconds for 100 yards. He was just a fair passer. In college, he completed 139 of 239 passes for 1,786 yards, a good but not an astounding mark. As a punter, he averaged 39.6 yards for his 85 kicks at SMU. He was a good blocker but seldom got the chance to block because his coaches did not want him to risk injury.

Yet Doak Walker had a faculty for producing the big play at the big moment. He was at his best under pressure. He was a climax player and he was so good that there are those who rate him as the greatest single player ever to come out of the Southwest Conference. "Some called it luck, others called it destiny — this young man had a natural knack for pulling off great deeds," said SMU head coach Matty Bell.

"It was his split vision," said TCU's Coach Dutch Meyer. "Doak had the greatest split vision I ever saw."

Whatever the qualities, they probably never were more impressively demonstrated than on the clear, mild Saturday afternoon in Fort Worth, November 29, 1947. Southern Methodist had won nine straight games and was ranked No. 2 nationally. Texas Christian's record was only half as good, 4–4–1, but the Horned Frogs were in a position to knock the Mustangs out of the Conference championship. SMU was a 13-point favorite.

Doak Walker was completing his second varsity year and already he had established himself as one of the Southwest's greats. As a freshman, he had been picked as the second best back in the Conference (his old teammate, Bobby Layne, was first) and he had been invited to the East–West Shrine game in San Francisco where he pitched a touchdown pass that tied the score, 6–6. Earlier in the 1947 season, he had faced Layne before 45,000 in Dallas and had led SMU to a 14–13 victory over Texas. Now the SMU–TCU game was the season's climax.

Texas Christian, led by a hard-working, keenly competitive quarterback named Lindy Berry, exploded for a quick 12–0 lead that stunned the crowd and rocked the favored and perhaps too complacent Mustangs back on their heels.

Only 5 minutes and 35 seconds had elapsed in the game when TCU found itself on the SMU 46 after an exchange of punts. On the first play, Berry whirled laterally to the right and threw a leaping pass deep into SMU territory. His target was Morris (Snake) Bailey, a rangy end. Bailey went high in the air with a cluster of SMU players, including Dick McKissack, Paul Page and Walker. Bailey, making a miraculous catch, came down with a thud on the SMU 14. Then the Frogs gave the

Lindy Berry, TCU's backfield star, in full stride

ball to their plunging fullback, Pete Stout. One time, two times, three times, and then on the fourth try he plunged over from the two for a touchdown. The kick failed and TCU led 6–0.

Doak Walker took Wayne Pitcock's ensuing kickoff three yards in the end zone and feinted like a boxer as he moved gracefully to the left side of the field. Changing pace, pointing out obstacles to his blockers but never getting much more than a yard from the sideline, Walker raced to the TCU 23 — a return of 77 yards before he was driven out-of-bounds. Paul Page picked up eight yards on two carries and Walker made it first down on the 12. Three pass plays failed. On fourth down, Walker took a handoff from Gil Johnson and completed a pass to Bobby Folsom at the TCU four. But it wasn't enough. TCU fans breathed easier when Carl Knox kicked out 56 yards.

Moments later, Orien Browning of TCU plucked off an SMU pass by Johnson which deflected off Walker's shoulder and, picking up a cordon of blockers, raced to the SMU one before being brought down by McKissack. The Mustangs held momentarily but Lindy Berry, on third down, shot a pass to Stout in the end zone. Again Pitcock's try for placement failed, and TCU led 12–0 in the opening moments of the second period.

Spirits were beginning to drop on the SMU side of the stands as the first half moved nearer the end with no further threat from the unbeaten Mustangs. Then with the clock reading 3:20 to go, Walker, trying to

Doak Walker runs 76 yards for a score

pass from his own 39, found himself trapped. He shook a phantom hip at a couple of TCU chargers. Then, squirming, feinting, stiff-arming, he picked his way through the open field 61 yards to a touchdown, scoring standing up. At the 23, Page took out one tackler. Walker outfoxed the safety man, Randy Rogers, just before hitting the goal line. Walker kicked the extra point that sent the players to half-time intermission with TCU leading 12–7.

TCU threatened three times in the third quarter. Rogers recovered a McKissack fumble on the 17 and the Horned Frogs moved to the SMU 11 before Page ended the threat by intercepting a pass in the end zone. Another time a wild pass from center rolled between Page and Walker, and Wayne Rogers recovered for TCU inside the 10-yard line. The SMU line threw back three thrusts, then on fourth down Walker knocked down a pass in the end zone. After a third TCU threat had been repulsed Frank Payne, Walker's understudy, punted to the SMU 33 and a roughness penalty against TCU moved the ball back to the 48. The Mustangs, with Walker at the throttle, moved resolutely downfield, covering the distance in thirteen plays and Walker scoring on an end run from the five. But Walker's kick failed and now the score read: SMU 13, TCU 12.

That's the way the score stood as the two teams battled through the remainder of the third period and through most of the fourth. Then came high drama in one of the Southwest Conference's most exciting football finishes.

The big clock showed exactly 90 seconds to go when the Horned Frogs of TCU, in their purple-and-white jerseys, broke out of the huddle on their own 20-yard line — third down and 20 to go. The Frogs went into one of their characteristic widespread formations with Lindy Berry back. Berry took the center pass, danced back a few steps and then cut loose a long, spiraling pass to Snake Bailey, racing down the field 35 yards from scrimmage. Bailey took the ball in full stride and, with his long legs pumping, headed toward the SMU goal. McKissack and Walker got solid hands on the gangling sophomore end, who lateraled the ball back to halfback Charlie Jackson, who broke off on a diagonal tangent. Walker got a piece of his jersey but it was Bobby Folsom who got the runner's legs, hitting him from the side and dropping him at the eight. The play covered 72 yards. On the first play, Berry took the snap and started to the right where he ran into a cordon of Mustangs. Berry tossed the ball back to fullback Pete Stout on the 10. Stout bobbled the ball. It rolled on the ground, a couple of Mustangs touched it, then Stout scooped it up and plunged across for a touchdown. SMU was bewildered. Wayne Pitcock, who had missed his first two conversion tries,

Gil Johnson, SMU's passing master

put one through the uprights this time and TCU led 19–13, with only seconds remaining.

In its exuberance at this quick and favorable turn, TCU must have lost some of its acumen. The following kickoff — a tragic blunder — went to Doak Walker, waiting with arms open at the eight-yard line. Doak obviously was leg-weary. He paused momentarily, just to plot his runback pattern, then flew toward the right sidelines. He evaded one tackler, then a second, then two more. His route carried him past the SMU bench. As he picked his way along the sideline — purple-and-white jerseys pouring down on him — Walker yelled to Coach Matty Bell, "Send Johnson in now!"

Finally, after a 57-yard return, Walker was brought down on the TCU 35 on a flying tackle by defensive man Randy Rogers. Less than a minute remained to play. Coach Bell, heeding Doak's suggestion on the run, rushed in Gil Johnson, his passing fireman. Bell delighted in telling of this incident years afterward. He would shake his head incredulously and remark, "Can you imagine that guy, with tacklers all around him, having the presence of mind to ask me to send in a special quarterback? It was typical of his poise and his quick thinking under fire."

With time precious, SMU went for the big bomb. Twice Johnson threw desperation passes into the end zone — first to Walker and then to Sid Halliday. Both were overthrown. On third down, Johnson shot a pass to Walker, who outfought a bunch of clawing TCU hands and caught the ball on the nine. The clock showed 25 seconds to play. Bell paced nervously in front of the SMU bench. Dutch Meyer pawed at the dirt on the TCU side. Occasionally he barked defensive instructions.

Then Johnson dropped back for the fourth time. Everybody in the stands was watching No. 37 — Doak Walker. So was the desperate TCU defense. Johnson rifled the ball to Halliday, the team captain, in the end zone.

The stadium was bedlam when a dusty, physically spent Walker went back to make the try for the extra point — and missed.

The Doaker

It was of no consequence. This was Doak Walker's day. Game statistics revealed that he had had kickoff returns of 77 and 57 yards. He had another run of 61 yards from scrimmage. He scored two touchdowns, accounted for 119 yards rushing, completed 10 of 14 passes for 136 yards, returned three kickoffs for a total of 163 yards and returned three punts for 53. Altogether, he had gained 471 yards.

"It was a great game," Dutch Meyer said afterward. "Walker was the difference."

Coach Bell said, "If this man isn't an All-American, there is no such thing."

A TCU tackle, Harold Kilman, a former Golden Gloves boxer, paid the highest tribute. "I learned when I was boxing to read a man's face," Kilman said. "I can tell by his eyes, his expression if he is beaten. During the SMU game, even when the Mustangs were a touchdown behind with only a minute to play, Walker never looked like a beaten man. He still had that confident, calm look of a man who expected to pull the fat out of the fire."

The tie clinched the Conference championship for SMU and the Mustangs went to the Cotton Bowl where they played Penn State to a 13-13 tie. Texas whipped Alabama 27-7 in the Sugar Bowl and TCU received an invitation to the Delta Bowl in Memphis, losing to the University of Mississippi 13-9.

There was one other bit of intriguing conversational side play following the dramatic SMU-TCU tie. After Doak Walker and the Mustangs had gained the tie in the fading seconds, Coach Dutch Meyer of TCU accosted his good friend, Coach Marty Bell of SMU, and said, "God is certainly with the Methodists this year."

"God is a Southern Methodist," Bell replied.

6

The Luck—and the Scare—
of the Irish

DECEMBER 3, 1949

NOTRE DAME	**27**
SOUTHERN METHODIST	**20**

A funereal atmosphere pervaded the Southern Methodist dressing room, Players donned their football armor without a word, their faces pale and their lips tight. Nerves were as taut as guitar strings. You could cut the mood with a rusty butcher knife.

Coach Matty Bell, wearing a weatherbeaten jacket turned up around the neck, headed for the door. He had taken only a few steps when Halfback Kyle Rote jumped up and approached him. "Let's go get 'em today, coach," Rote said. He extended his right hand.

Bell, a look of surprise on his face, reached out for the handshake.

"Bzzz-zzz-zzz!"

The coach jumped back quickly, stiffened, and there was a brief moment of startled silence throughout the room. Rote's right hand had concealed one of those trick hand buzzers which give out with a buzz and a shock.

Then Bell burst into a broad grin. So did Rote. The room, still and solemn minutes before, echoed with good-natured laughter. "What a riot!" someone yelled. The players guffawed. Tension was broken.

"I don't know why I did it," Rote recalled. "It was a goofy thing to do. It was just an impulse, I guess."

For the Mustangs of Southern Methodist University, that little locker room episode was about the only thing to smile about on that sodden, forbidding day of December 3, 1949.

Coach Frank Leahy and his Fighting Irish of Notre Dame had come to Dallas for what appeared to be little more than a warm-up. It looked

Emil "Six-Yard" Sitko of Notre Dame

Notre Dame's great coach Frank Leahy

as if it would be a crime — sadistic cruelty — to send anything but the Irish third-stringers onto the field. This was the mighty machine which Leahy later was to term his greatest at Notre Dame. Piling onto an awesome string of thirty-eight games without a loss over four seasons, this particular team had swept to nine straight triumphs. It had scored 49 touchdowns and piled up 333 points. It was ranked No. 1 nationally. It had made mincemeat of all opposition, its closest test having been a 34–21 victory over always troublesome Michigan State.

Bob Williams was the quarterback. The fullback was Steve Sitko — "Six-yard Sitko," they called him, because that was his average per carry. Frank Spaniel and Larry Coutre, with fourteen touchdowns between them, were the halfbacks. The line was anchored by All-America tackle Jim Martin. The most frightening man on the team, however, was end Leon Hart, six-six, 260 pounds, the "Monster of Turtle Creek, Pennsylvania," later to receive the Heisman Trophy as the best college football player of the year. "The greatest football machine of modern times," said the sportswriters.

If it had been a fight, the authorities wouldn't have permitted it. If the players had been horses or dogs instead of human beings, the game certainly would have incurred the intervention of the Society for the Prevention of Cruelty to Animals.

"It's like stopping General Pershing tanks with M–1 rifles," wrote Felix R. McKnight in the Dallas *News*, using the military jargon of the day.

The Mustangs, indeed, appeared to be a scrawny, pitiful lot when measured beside the behemoths from South Bend. Their season's record was lackluster. In their nine previous games, they had given up 47 points in losing to Rice and had been battered also by Baylor, 35–26, and Texas Christian, 21–13. They had tied Texas A&M, 27–27.

At full strength, Southern Methodist had scant right to be on the same field with Notre Dame, but the Methodists were well below their physical best. Their star quarterback, Doak Walker, had a pulled muscle in his right leg and didn't even suit up for the game. Also injured were Halfback Frank Payne, Guard Herbie Wales and Tackle Bobby Vann. Another tackle, Bobby Collier, was only 50 per cent effective.

The football cards listed the Mustangs as 28-point underdogs. It apparently was just a figure pulled out of the clouds. It might as well have been 55 points.

The crowd of 75,457 came out primarily for a look at Notre Dame's celebrated stars — Sitko, Hart, Williams, Martin. Even the most loyal of them didn't dare hope that the battered Mustangs could make a fight of it.

After Rote's hand buzzer trick had cracked the tension, Matty Bell's youngsters suddenly took on an air that looked nothing like cattle being prepared for the slaughter.

Doak Walker, in civilian clothes, stood up in a chair and told his teammates, "I would give my right arm to be playing today. This is a great honor and a great challenge. You can do it, men."

Mike Brumbelow, a former Texas Christian and Mississippi line coach who had scouted Notre Dame as a favor to Bell, said, "These guys are not ogres. You can beat 'em."

It was a grim but inspired Southern Methodist team that charged onto the field — yelling and whooping and slapping each other on the padded sections.

Frank Leahy, on the other side of the field, might have seen this demonstration and gulped a little, giving his perennial bow tie a wiggle. If so, it's certain, he looked at his appointed victims benignly.

He must have fidgeted, however, when the first nine minutes went by without Notre Dame getting a first down. Sure, Southern Methodist was fired up. The Texans, outweighed up to twenty pounds man-for-man in some spots, were hitting and fighting hard. This was only natural, realists conceded, but soon they would wear down and then would come the mountainslide. The Irish also were a bit too overconfident. You could count on the astute Leahy to fix that.

Then — boom — it happened. Williams shot a pass to end Bill

Bill Wightkin of Notre Dame gets behind Rote for a superb catch to set up an Irish touchdown

Wightkin, good for 42 yards and a touchdown. Steve Oracko converted. Notre Dame led, 7–0. People settled back for the rout.

With Doak Walker out of the lineup, Southern Methodist's fortunes were vested in Kyle Rote, playing tailback, and a 168-pound string of gristle named Johnny Champion, at halfback.

Rote was born in Odessa, Texas. His father, Jack, was a WPA worker. Rote played at Thomas Jefferson High School in San Antonio and at SMU he performed in the shadow of the great Walker, who was a year ahead of him. Rote was not an outstanding passer, but he was a wonderful runner, possessing speed and deception. He had tremendously quick hands and was an excellent pass receiver.

Champion was small and gutty. He did some passing but he was at his best on defense. His target for the day was the giant Leon Hart.

The first time Southern Methodist had the ball, Hart charged in from end like an enraged bull. Champion hit him low, around the ankles, and Hart fell on his face, as if tripped by a piece of rope. He got up dazed and gave Champion a quizzical look. People just didn't do that to Leon Hart.

Moments later, Hart moved his 280 pounds again toward the action. Plop! Again he went sprawling. And there was the five-six, 168-pound Champion wrapped aound the big Irish end's legs like a coiled wire.

This happened time and time again. Once Hart picked himself off the ground, wagged a finger under Champion's nose and warned, "If you hold me again, I'll tell the referee on you."

Champion only smiled. When Hart's back was turned, Johnny stuck out his tongue at the giant as would a spiteful kid. Champion's artful job on the massive and greatly feared Hart plus the aggressive play of the entire SMU team made it quite obvious that the nation's top football power was not in for a Dallas picnic.

This became more manifest early in the second period. Trailing 7–0, Southern Methodist caught the Fighting Irish off guard and Champion hit on a 78-yard pass to Zohn Milam, moving to the Irish five. Rote carried the ball to the Notre Dame one while the stands went crazy. But there the Irish held.

As if stung by this insolence, the Irish stormed back moments later and drove 66 yards to another score, capped by a 35-yard pass from Williams to Ernie Zalejski. It was a weird play. Zalejski was surrounded by three SMU men — Billy Richards, Bob Folsom and Milam. One of them tapped the ball into Zalejski's hands near the goal line and he went over. The point was missed, and the two teams went to intermission with Notre Dame leading, 13–0. None was more astonished at the closeness of the score than Leahy and the Irish themselves.

The Mustangs were a spirited bunch in the dressing room at the half. They felt now that they could give the Irish a game. Doak Walker made another short speech. So did Brumbelow who, with Bell and assistant coach Rusty Russell, pointed out some of Notre Dame's weaknesses and

Johnny Champion and Kyle Rote
coping with an impossible lie

Pat Knight blocks as Kyle Rote breaks a tackle to score for SMU

outlined means of exploiting them. "We can beat 'em," Brumbelow repeated.

The psychological stimulus at the half had its effect on the out-manned SMU team. Shortly after the second period opened, Rote engineered a 71-yard drive that scored in five plays. The boyish-looking tailback personally accounted for all but 18 of the yards and he slipped around right end for the score. Pat Knight led blockers in opening a gaping hole, and it was easy. Bill Sullivan kicked the point and Notre Dame's lead was cut to 13–7.

This was a sharp blow to the Irish pride. Leahy, his smile gone, could be seen gesticulating in front of the Notre Dame bench. Players slapped their padded knees. Irish confidence was shaken, but the South Benders responded as champions should.

A few minutes later, Rote dropped back to pass from his own 24. He was rushed. The ball fell into a cluster of Notre Dame and SMU hands and when officials had separated the jerseys it was Notre Dame's end James Mutscheller who had the ball on the Mustang 22. Halfback Bill Barrett scored from four yards out. The conversion was made and Notre Dame now led 20–7.

This was the time for the Mustangs to fold. They didn't. Instead, they hit back twice as hard and rocked the Irish with a second touchdown early in the fourth period. This was another lightning strike.

SMU took the kickoff on its own 29. Young Rusty Russell, Jr., son of the Mustangs' backfield coach, was calling plays from the open huddle, Notre Dame style, and although a sophomore was doing a superb job of it.

"We decided that since we didn't have Walker in there we would use the open huddle," Bell explained later. "There might be a tendency toward volunteer quarterbacking. We didn't want anybody talking back."

Young Russell was not the kind of lad to brook any backtalk or sass from his teammates, anyhow. He didn't even listen to his own father and his coach.

"I tried to give him some plays but I soon discovered he was calling the shots better than I could from the press box," the elder Russell said. "So I left him alone."

With Doak Walker not in the SMU lineup, the Irish were jamming up their defense and not guarding too much against the pass. Young Russell and the SMU coaches noticed that Notre Dame was disinclined to change its defense even when a pass was successful.

Russell called a pass. Rote threw to Henry Stollenwerck, but it was

Leon Hart, Notre Dame's All-American end and occasional fullback

Quarterback Bob Williams of Notre Dame

only good for two yards. Notre Dame's defense lined up the same way. Russell called another pass. This time, Rote shot the ball to Champion, who grabbed it at his own 34, angled to the left sideline and scooted toward the Notre Dame goal as fast as his bandy legs could carry him. The Irish were caught napping, but Notre Dame guard Bob Lally, with a tremendous effort, managed to nail Champion at the one-foot line. The play was good for 64 yards. This time Notre Dame couldn't hold. Rote carried over center and Sullivan converted to make the score 20–14.

By this time, there was bedlam in the pro-SMU stands. Leahy walked nervously up and down in front of the Notre Dame bench, calling small conferences with players and assistant coaches. There was little aplomb left on the SMU side of the field.

Bell had a closed-circuit TV set placed in a weatherproof metal box behind the SMU bench for monitoring purposes. Herman Cowley, assistant coach, was the man designated to watch the screen and make suggestions for substitutions and player deployment.

Once he got so excited watching the game that he failed to sub for a man and SMU was left with ten men on the field.

With the score now 20–14, it was obvious to everyone that SMU was in a position to win the game and pull off the greatest football upset of the century.

The Methodists kicked off, and a clipping penalty put the Irish back on their one. Barrett once was almost dropped for a safety. Williams punted to Billy Richards on the Notre Dame 43 and Richards hauled the ball back to the 14. On the next play, Rote swept left end, and weaving in and out of the hands of tacklers, appeared to have gone into the end zone for a touchdown standing up.

The crowd went mad. But suddenly there was a hush. An official, waving his arms, called the ball back and placed it on the four. Spirits sank. Rote's foot had stepped out-of-bounds, the official ruled. The crowd recalled how the mighty Irish had stopped an earlier charge at the one.

Rote hit the line for two of the four yards and then raced around right end for the remainder. Touchdown! The score was tied 20–20. But SMU had a chance to take the lead on a conversion. It remained only a chance. Jerry Groom, the big Irish center, rushed in and blocked Sullivan's kick. The score remained tied with 12 minutes remaining.

The Irish were mad. The Mustangs were elated, but tired. Notre Dame was still the country's No. 1 team and intended to prove it — the hard, murderous way. Moments later, the Irish took the ball on their own 43 and drove 57 yards to a touchdown.

They didn't do it mercifully. They chewed up the ground in small chunks, boring their way through SMU's plucky but battered defenses. Barrett went for eight yards. Six-yard Sitko kept his franchise. He got six. Francis Spaniel added four. In desperation, the Irish pulled the giant Hart back from end and threw him in at fullback. Hart plunged six yards. So it went until finally Dick Barrett knifed across from the six, crossing the line at the coffin corner. Oracko's kick was through the middle, and Notre Dame led 27–20.

Johnny Champion, No. 15, rises from ground to watch Kyle Rote breaking to his right with Leon Hart and Bob Toneff in pursuit

The game wasn't over. Southern Methodist smashed back and, behind the running of Rote, Stollenwerck and Champion, drove to the Notre Dame four-yard line, with seconds remaining to play. The clock was running out when, on a fourth down play, Rote spotted Champion in the end zone. He rifled a pass. Notre Dame's Jerry Groom made a desperate lunge and just barely managed to deflect it.

The ball — and SMU's hopes for a tie and an upset — went trickling away into the dusk. The crowd was left limp from the excitement. SMU didn't manage to knock off the nation's No. 1 football power but it came close and it wrote a chapter in Southwest football history that never will be forgotten.

"I was watching the Notre Dame bench," Bell recalled later. "There was pandemonium. They went crazy."

The SMU players, realizing they had given a magnificent performance, walked into the dressing room in high spirits, many of them smiling broadly.

All but one. That was Rote. He was crying unashamedly.

Walker came over to Rote and wrapped his arms around the player who had so brilliantly filled his shoes that day. "I love you, boy," Walker said.

Father John J. Cavanagh, Notre Dame president, paid a special visit to the SMU dressing room.

"We of Notre Dame want to congratulate you," he said to Coach Bell and the Mustang players. "It was the most terrific game we have had in several years."

"If we'd had the Doaker, we'd have won," mumbled a disappointed SMU lineman.

He probably wouldn't have said it if he had thought it was any reflection on Rote, who filled in so admirably. Rote scored all three SMU touchdowns. He accounted for 115 yards running and 146 yards passing. He was the day's individual standout, although special praise also went to little Johnny Champion, who gained 117 yards through pass receptions; defensive end Pat Knight and tackle Neal Franklin.

In addition to his passing-catching heroics, Champion distinguished himself as the bane of Notre Dame's giant Leon Hart.

"The first time I blocked him, he went sprawling," Champion said afterward. "Mr. Hart and I had an understanding right there."

"Six-yard" Sitko gained 84 yards in fourteen carries, exactly his quota. Rote outpunted his rival, Williams, averaging 48 yards to Williams', 38.5. The closeness of the battle was emphasized in the statistics. SMU had 18 first downs to 16 for the Irish, gained 102 yards rushing to Notre Dame's 277, but piled up 307 yards in the air against the winner's 165.

Steve Oracko, the Notre Dame guard and place-kicker, had praise for Rote. "That Rote runs right down your throat," he said.

Frank Leahy, Jr., son of the Notre Dame coach, came by the SMU dressing room. He said he wanted two autographs — Rote and Walker.

Matty Bell, reassessing the game, acknowledged that Rote played one of his greatest games and that the entire SMU team gave everything it had. However, he saved some credit for his free-lance scout, Mike Brumbelow.

"I knew Mike was one of the best scouts in the business, but he wasn't in football any more," the SMU coach later related. "I called him up one day and I said, 'Mike, I want you to do a job for me.' He asked what it was and I told him. He said he couldn't get away from his business.

"I told him I wanted him to scout five Notre Dame games for me and also work with the boys the week of the game. I said I'd pay him $125 a week and expenses. That was a lot of money. The going rate was $60 a week. He agreed.

"He did one whale of a job. He knew every movement that the Notre Dame team made. He knew every weakness and every strength. He showed pictures. He suggested tactics. He got the boys to believing they could win."

Bell said it was decided that the Mustangs would be unable to run inside Notre Dame's tackles.

"We decided to use spread formations and concentrate on forward passes and wide runs," he added. "We just threw the long passes enough to keep them honest."

After the game, Notre Dame's Coach Leahy, never losing his poise, adjusted his bow tie and addressed his assembled athletes:

"You are my greatest team — God bless you every one. Something happened today for which we've prayed. We have now what they call the national championship. Perhaps you think that calls for celebration. Before you celebrate, I want each of you to write a letter to your parents, thanking them for sending you to Notre Dame. Then I want you to go to the Holy Trinity Church and show your gratitude to God."

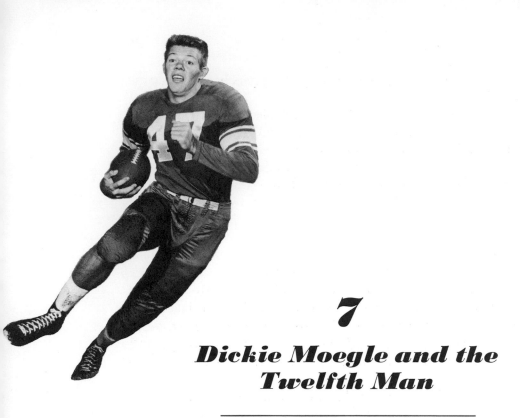

7

Dickie Moegle and the Twelfth Man

COTTON BOWL: JANUARY 1, 1954

RICE   28
ALABAMA   6

Whenever Texans gather to talk about unforgettable moments of Southwest Conference football, the conversation inevitably drifts back to the day that little Dicky Moegle ran wild for Rice against Alabama and it took a freak play by an illegal twelfth man to bring him to earth.

The startling act of an Alabama player leaping impulsively off the bench to head off the Rice left halfback, who was in full flight and goalward bound, produced a strange psychological effect on both teams. Rice became fighting mad. Alabama was ashamed and completely demoralized. The result was an overwhelming 28–6 Rice victory, but the score fails to encompass the dramatics of that fantastic afternoon.

It was the Cotton Bowl game in Dallas, January 1, 1954. Rice and Texas had finished the regular season atop the Southwest Conference with similar 5–1 records but the Owls received the bowl bid because they had beaten the Longhorns 18–13. Rice's over-all record was 8–2, with losses to Southern Methodist and Kentucky. Alabama's Crimson Tide, under Coach Harold (Red) Drew had come off a spotty campaign with losses to Mississippi Southern and Maryland and ties with Tennessee,

Louisiana State and Mississippi State. The men from Tuscaloosa were determined to atone for their mediocre season with an impressive Cotton Bowl victory.

They had the weapons. Up front was a massive line with plenty of muscle. The backfield presented a double attacking threat in Corky Tharp, an excellent runner, and Bart Starr, a smart quarterback with a good arm.

Rice had a good but not an overpowering team. It featured a savage ground game built around an All-America fullback, Dave (Kosse) Johnson, who ran like a halfback, and Moegle, a 167-pound will-o'-the-wisp who had the speed of a frightened deer. Alabama knew it need not worry about passes. Rice had no passer of note and rotated quarterback duties among LeRoy Fenstemaker, Buddy Grantham, Atchley Proctor and sophomore Pinky Nisbett.

The Owls were a one-touchdown favorite, principally on their superior season's record. Even their staunchest supporters feared, however, they would be in for a rocky, and perhaps losing, afternoon. Their offense had been built around the hard-running Johnson, who had led the conference in rushing with 944 yards and in scoring with 62 points. Two weeks before the Cotton Bowl game, the Rice fullback had torn up a

Backfield star Kosse Johnson of Rice

knee in scrimmage and there was question whether he could stand up long under the pounding of the big and aggressive Crimson linemen. The fear proved well-founded.

Rice still had one ace in the hole. That was Jess Neely, the gaunt, steely-eyed head coach who had proven to be a master of trap plays. "Give old Jess a few good boys up front and he'll trap you to death," one rival coach said. Alabama, beefy but slow, appeared to be a setup for such tactics.

A sellout crowd of 75,504 showed up in bright, crisp weather for the eighteenth Cotton Bowl game. Texas Governor Allen Shivers appeared, chatting with friends and waving amiably to his constituents. A conspicuous absentee was Governor Gordon Persons of Alabama. Persons was an Auburn graduate. He chose to watch Auburn play Texas Tech in the Gator Bowl at Jacksonville, Florida.

Kosse Johnson, the Rice fullback, started the game with a heavily taped knee. He was a marked man. Time after time, as he sought to run with the ball, he was hit by a swarm of red jerseys. The game was 10 minutes, 49 seconds old when Johnson fell writhing to the ground. He was carried off the field, not to return to the game. The despair of Rice's supporters permeated the stands.

The loss of Johnson put the fate of the Owls squarely in the hands of Moegle. This was a spindle-legged youngster who looked as if he might have wandered in from the neighborhood park. He had entered college at an early age and now, although a junior, he had just reached his eighteenth birthday.

Rice's hopes sagged deeply a few moments after Johnson's departure when Alabama struck for the first touchdown of the game. Bart Starr intercepted a LeRoy Fenstemaker pass on the Rice 49 to give the Tide a break. Tommy Lewis, the Alabama fullback, hammered away at the Rice line. In seven plays, Alabama was over for a touchdown, Lewis plunging from the one. John Hudson, Rice guard, partly blocked Bubby Luna's attempted kick but the Tide led, 6–0.

Rice's John Hudson, outstanding guard

The game moved into the second period, and still Rice failed to muster a charge. Coach Neely became impatient. He paced up and down in front of his bench and then spoke out, addressing no one in particular, "Have I got a quarterback who can go in there and get that ball across the goal line?" There was a slight pause.

"I can, coach." Neely turned sharply and looked into the eyes of the speaker. It was a skinny sub quarterback named Buddy Grantham.

"Get in there!" Neely ordered. Grantham ran eagerly into the huddle and Fenstemaker, who had handled the team through the first period, trotted unhappily to the bench.

"Forty-three trap!" Grantham barked, calling his first signal. He clapped his hands and the Owls lined up on the ball, resting on the Rice 21. Grantham faked handoffs to the right halfback, Gordon Kellogg, and to Mac Taylor, the fullback who had gone in as a sub for Johnson. John Hudson, Rice's All-America left guard, trapped the Alabama guard. Grantham slipped the ball to Moegle, who burst between the trapped Alabama guard and the center.

When he crossed the scrimmage line, Moegle hit open country, because Alabama, with disdain for Rice's pass potential, was using an eight-man line. Moegle outran the Tide linebacker and now had only two red jerseys between him and the goal line. Moegle picked up one of his ends, Blois Bridges, who threw a perfect block at the first of the two remaining Alabama defenders. Then he slowed his pace and fell behind his other end, Dan Hart, who neatly took out the safety man. Moegle cut away from his pursuers and raced down the sideline to a touchdown — 79 yards.

One couldn't hear himself scream when Fenstemaker came in to kick the extra point, putting Rice ahead 7–6.

Alabama struck back like a wounded cougar. With Bart Starr passing and Lewis hitting the line, the Tide marched to the Rice 10. There, however, Starr lost the ball on a fumble and Rice took over. Then came a five-yard penalty against the Owls. They looked up the field and there were 95 long yards to go.

Fenstemaker had returned to the Rice quarterback role. Deep in his own territory, he called what appeared to be the logical play — a fullback smash into the middle — but wasn't. He faked the ball to Mac Taylor, then handed off to Moegle, sweeping across from left halfback. John Hudson and a 6-foot-6 tackle named Dick Chapman opened a gaping hole, and the nimble-footed Moegle was through it like a flash. For a moment it appeared that Alabama's linebacker might plug the gap but Moegle gave him a head fake and left him standing in his cleated shoes as he broke into the clear.

Fullback
Mac Taylor of Rice

As in his earlier 79-yard run, the little Rice halfback picked up his blockers and headed down the field. Guard Kenny Paul pulled out and cut down the Alabama end. Halfback Gordon Kellogg threw a perfect block at the defensive left halfback. Center Leo Rucka raced into the secondary to take care of the Alabama defensive half. When Dan Hart again took out the Tide safety man, Moegle had nothing ahead of him but fresh air — about 60 yards. He cut to the sideline — Alabama's side of the field — and shot toward the goal, his little legs moving like those of a runaway pony.

Then it happened — like something from a movie screen. As Moegle raced past the Alabama bench, a figure in a crimson jersey spurted onto the field, hit the little Rice halfback from the blind side and sent him sprawling to the field.

At first there was a moment of shocked silence. Then consternation. Then bedlam. The stands buzzed with excitement. The players of both benches jumped to their feet. Neely, the normally mild-mannered Rice coach, crossed the field and could be seen arguing heatedly and shaking a finger under the nose of the big, red-haired coach of the Tide. Eddie Wojecki, the Rice trainer, rushed onto the field and began working over the prostrate form of Moegle, who appeared at first to be badly hurt.

By this time, the impact of the deed had reached home with the incensed and highly partisan crowd, which began to yell, "Kill him! Throw the bum out!"

The man who made the tackle — his face redder now than his jersey — turned out to be Tommy Lewis, twenty-year-old senior, the regular fullback and captain of the Alabama team.

Tommy Lewis of Alabama

He sheepishly scurried back to the bench, buried his face in his hands and began to sob hysterically. "I don't know why I did it — I just don't know why I did it," Lewis kept repeating over and over after the game. "I'm just too emotional, I guess. I'm too full of Alabama. When Dicky came down the sidelines next to our bench, I thought of just one thing — I've got to stop him."

For a few moments after the bizarre incident it appeared that the game might develop into a riot. But referee Cliff Shaw acted quickly and positively. He picked up the football, ran to the Alabama goal line, put the ball down and raised his arms in the traditional signal of a touchdown.

A loud roar erupted from the crowd. There was no protest from Coach Red Drew and the Alabama bench — only silence and embarrassment. For Moegle it was a 95-yard touchdown run and for Rice, with the extra point, it was a 14–6 lead.

"I think it was fair," Moegle said afterward. "I don't think anyone

76

LEWIS (A)

MOEGLE (R)

DeLAURENTIS (A)

OLIVER (A)

CHAPMAN (R)

*Tommy Lewis rushes from the bench to tackle Dickie Moegle, as Moegle
appears to be touchdown bound*

could have caught me." He forgave easily. "I am sorrier than I can say for Tommy. I am positive his action was on the spur of the moment. I don't think he had any thought of injuring anyone."

Bob Rule, who covered the game for the Houston *Press,* said he wasn't sure that it was an impetuous act. "I was watching Lewis almost from the time the play developed," Rule said. "As Moegle shifted for position and headed toward the sideline, I saw Lewis grab a headgear. The tackle looked planned to me."

The crowd may have thought so, too, for a while. It remained in an ugly mood, yelling for the Rice players to "Tear 'em up!" Many continued to boo Lewis, who remained on the bench with his head in his arms. The Rice players, even though awarded the touchdown, appeared bitter.

An old-fashioned rock-sock bloodletting might have been in the offing had not the cool and resourceful referee, Cliff Shaw, acted again. As the Rice players walked down the field to kick the extra point, Shaw approached Dan Hart, Rice end and co-captain and said, "Dan, we can either have a good football game for the rest of the afternoon or we can have trouble. When you fellows come up to the line of scrimmage, why don't you shake hands with the Alabama linemen and tell them to forget the incident and let's play football."

Hart passed the message on to his teammates and they readily agreed. Not many people in the stands saw it but when the teams lined up for the extra point, the Owls made their conciliatory gesture. The Tide players reacted with a grin. Tension eased. The remainder of the game was played without incident.

At the half, Lewis went directly to the Rice dressing room where he apologized, first to Coach Neely, then the player. He especially singled out Moegle who told him, "Forget it." Neely was touched. "My heart went out to that boy," the Rice coach said. "I told him, 'Don't let it bother you.' "

Although tension and crowd demonstrations subsided, the game took a sharp turn in the second half. The Rice team became a determined and deadly machine. The heart went out of Alabama. The Tide merely went through the paces the rest of the way.

In the third period — with about ten minutes gone — Moegle mustered the Owls on another drive, this one covering 67 yards, and climaxed it by sweeping around end for 34 yards and his third touchdown. Fenstemaker converted and Rice led 21–6, but the damage had not been fully done.

Late in the third period, with the tired regulars on the bench, Rice's second team launched another march that was to carry 75 yards and over into the fourth period. Buddy Grantham engineered the march and scored himself on a bootleg play from the seven-yard line. Sammie Burk kicked the point and that was the scoring for the day, 28–6.

Before the game ended, Lewis was reinserted into the Alabama lineup by Coach Drew and the fullback got a tremendous ovation from the crowd. But try as he might, Lewis was unable to push through his savage smashes at the line his teammates needed, to get back into the ball game; and Starr could not find a way to penetrate Rice's secondary again.

It was Rice's day and Moegle's hour. The scrawny halfback with the speeding legs, remarkable poise and supersensitive vision gave one of the greatest individual performances in bowl football annals. His personal chart showed touchdown runs of 79, 95 and 34 yards. He gained 265 of his team's 379 yards on the ground. In the 11 times he carried the ball, he averaged 24.1 yards a clip. After the game, he held four Cotton Bowl records and three all-time records for bowl competition.

No one else compared with him for one-man heroics. Grantham, the sub Rice quarterback, hit on three of his five pass attempts for 43 yards. Dan Hart, the end, was a standout in the Rice line which also included outstanding performances by Ken Paul, John Hudson and Dick Chapman. They were largely responsible for holding Alabama's offense in

Bart Starr, before his days at Green Bay

check both on the ground and in the air. Bart Starr was able to complete only 7 of 16 passes for 67 yards. The Tide's chief groundgainer was Bill Oliver, held to 56 yards.

A spectator at the game was Doak Walker. Walker was impressed with the play of Moegle of whom he said, "He's exceptionally fast, very good at following blockers and has an uncanny knack for knowing the right time to cut. He's a wonderful back."

Perhaps more than Moegle's spectacular running, the 1954 Cotton Bowl will be remembered more for the impromptu tackle from the bench by Tommy Lewis, a play overshadowed in bowl history only perhaps by Roy Riegels' notorious wrong-way run in the 1929 Rose Bowl game. In that one, Riegels, of the University of California, grabbed a ball that had popped out of the hands of a Georgia Tech back and, after scampering around for a while, raced 60 yards to the wrong goal line. The resultant safety gave Georgia Tech an 8–7 victory and Riegels an unforgettable spot in football history. Undoubtedly, Tommy Lewis will find it equally hard to shake the memory.

After the incident, the Dallas *Morning News,* in an editorial written by managing editor Felix R. McKnight, urged Texans to try to ease the Alabama fullback's pain. "Drop Tommy Lewis a line," McKnight said in the editorial. "Let him know he hasn't lost his last friend. He committed a forgivable error that will live with him forever. He's quite a fighter . . . and we like them that way in Texas."

Lewis didn't return to Tuscaloosa with his teammates immediately. He remained in Dallas with a couple of his closest companions and tried vainly to shake the nightmare. He said later he couldn't do it. The reason he made the tackle, he said, was that he was stricken with a sudden impulse. "I couldn't relish the thought of losing."

But Alabama had lost and it was Dickie Moegle of Rice who ran to glory.

8

The Aggies Scored While the Bear Prayed

NOVEMBER 13, 1955

TEXAS A&M	20
RICE	12

The sixty-eight thousand spectators in the Rice Stadium at Houston were bored and restless. Scores of them moved toward the exits and into the parking lots. Only a little more than three minutes were left in the game and the die obviously had been cast. Rice led 12–0. Coach Paul (Bear) Bryant's so-called "Junction Boys" and the great John David Crow had been thoroughly throttled by the tough Rice defense. They were going nowhere in a tremendous hurry.

The boredom had wended its way to the spacious press box, overlooking the chalk-lined field. Some of the writers, the morning newspapermen, already were banging out their stories. Others leaned on their typewriters, sipped coffee from paper cups and indulged in small talk foreign to the game at hand. The game had offered little in the way of dramatics.

"Well, Mickey, you better be getting down to the dressing rooms," Clark Nealon, sports editor of the Houston *Post* said to the small, dark-haired man at his elbow.

"I know, and I'd rather take a beating than face Bryant," replied Mickey Herskowitz, the reporter assigned to the Aggies for post-game coverage.

"Why?" asked Nealon curiously.

"You know the Bear," said Mickey. "He's very superstitious and he'll blame that big story I did on him this morning for getting beat. He'll chew me out for jinxing him."

Rice had just scored its second touchdown and stretched its lead to 12–0. The clock showed 3:40 left. Herskowitz assembled his papers, watched the Rice kickoff deep in Aggie territory and then headed for the press box elevator. As the lumbersome lift drifted slowly and laboriously toward the ground floor, a loud roar was heard from the crowd. "Sounds like Rice recovered a fumble," Herskowitz said, shaking his shoulders resignedly.

The elevator was still dropping groundward when the air outside was split by another roar. "Guess Rice scored," Herskowitz said. Other locker room assignees on the elevator shook their heads in agreement.

When the elevator reached the ground, Herskowitz and the others elbowed their way through the standing crowd to get a glimpse of the field. Just as they reached the edge of the stadium, they saw Don Watson of the Aggies knife across for the touchdown. "Well, the Aggies at least scored," Herskowitz said. Then he glanced quickly at the score-board. To his amazement he saw the electric lights flash: "A&M 20, Rice 12."

By the time Herskowitz had battled his way to the Aggies' dressing room, the game was over and the weary players in their maroon-and-white jerseys were moving toward their lockers. Coach Bear Bryant was sitting on the steps, his head buried in his arms.

"What in the world happened, coach?" Herskowitz asked.

"I don't know," Bryant replied, "I was too busy praying."

The Aggies had pulled out the game by scoring three touchdowns in the space of two minutes and 18 seconds. It was one of the most unbelievable finishes in a Conference renowned for wild, unpredictable climaxes.

Paul (Bear) Bryant, head coach of A&M

The Aggies had gone into the game a one-touchdown favorite. After losing the opening game to UCLA 21–0, A&M scored successive victories over Louisiana State, Houston, Nebraska, Texas Christian and Baylor, tied Arkansas and edged Southern Methodist.

Rice, on the other hand, had started strongly, beating Alabama 20–0, tying Louisiana State 20–20 and trouncing Clemson 21–7. Then, inexplicably, the Owls seemed to come apart at the seams. They lost their fourth start to Southern Methodist 20–0, then dropped consecutive games to Texas, Kentucky and Arkansas. There were growing mumblings of discontent among Rice alumni and supporters when the veteran coach, Jess Neely, took the team into the game with the high-riding Aggies.

The wheelhorse of the A&M juggernaut was a six-two, 215-pound All-America back named Jim Crow. He was a fifty-minute performer. He was a punishing runner. He backed up the line and played safety. "John David gives so much of himself without regard for his physical wellbeing," Coach Bryant said, always reverently using his star's double name. "He's the greatest player I ever coached."

The Owls keyed on Crow and the big, racehorse back was held in check throughout most of the game. The contest was played in muggy weather, seventy-five-degree temperature, with steam rising from the wet turf.

The first three periods were a slugging match. Despite the presence of big John Crow and hard-running fullback Jack Pardee, the Aggies never got within sniffing distance of the goal line. Rice put on a con-

John David Crow of Texas A&M

King Hill of Rice

certed 56-yard drive in the third period, going to the Aggie 10 but there the drive died.

The game's long scoring drought finally was broken about one-third of the way through the final period. Rice took advantage of a short Aggie punt and went for a touchdown. King Hill scored from the eight but Jerry Hall's try for the extra point failed and Rice led, 6–0.

Then things started happening quickly. On the following kickoff, Bill Dendy of A&M fumbled and Lew Harpold recovered for Rice on the Aggies' 31. By this time, tempers on both sides had grown short and the hitting became fierce. You could almost hear the bones rattle in the contact at the line. Marshall Crawford of Rice suffered an injured knee and had to be helped to the sidelines. The Aggies' Roger Hobson went down under a pile and had to be carried from the field, not to return.

With the seconds ticking away, Rice moved briskly to its second touchdown. Paul Zipperlen took a pitchout and raced 14 yards. Short stabs at the line moved to the five. Zipperlen again took a pitchout and slashed across for the score. Dee Powell of the Aggies blocked the try for conversion but Rice now had what appeared to be — in view of the dogged defensive play — a relatively safe 12–0 lead. The clock showed nine minutes left.

The Aggies took the kickoff on their 37. Time and time again they shot Crow and Pardee into the line but the Owls piled up every charge. Once Jean Barras of the Owls banged into Crow with such force that the Aggie halfback crumbled to the ground and didn't get up. He was carried off the field. Now the Aggies were faced with an almost impos-

Jack Pardee, hard runner of A&M　　　　　*The Aggies' Lord Taylor*

sible situation — behind 12–0 and their best ballcarrier on the sidelines.

Into the game for the Aggies came Loyd Taylor. He was a third-stringer with little experience behind him. He had played the season in the shadow of Crow and Pardee. But — unspectacularly as he might have been, not especially fast, not particularly quick and too small to be powerful — he was the man who brought the sagging Aggies to life.

On an exchange of punts, Taylor took the ball on his own 42-yard line, veered to the sideline and raced 55 yards behind superb blocking to the Rice three. Bobby Keith and Gene Stallings threw effective blocks to aid the spectacular run. This was the time the first loud roar reached Mickey Herskowitz' ears in the press box elevator.

Two line plunges made only two yards. With third down and a yard to go, Taylor went over for the score. The conversion was good and Rice's margin had been cut to 12–7.

With only 3:18 left to play, the Aggies could not afford to give up possession of the football. This called for one of football's desperate but always dangerous maneuvers — the onside kick. Rice knew it was coming. Only one man played deep and the other ten members of the team were crammed up close to their own 40-yard line.

Jack Powell got off a good short kick for the Aggies. The ball took a crazy spin and began bouncing around the Rice 40 with players of both sides attempting to snare it. Gene Stallings, the A&M end and the man destined later to become coach of a winning Aggie team, was the lucky one. He made a leap and got the ball at the Rice 43. "I just wanted to get down there and knock somebody out of the way," Stallings, an end, explained later. "There was the ball, and I pounced on it."

On the first play from scrimmage — so quick that even the spectators were stunned — the Aggies had their second touchdown. Jimmy Wright got the ball and rifled a pass to Taylor, who had sped past the defender, Paul Zipperlen, and got into the clear. He took the ball over his left shoulder and raced across the goal line — a 43-yard strike.

The kick was good and the Aggies led 14–12. Another roar went up — and the elevator hadn't reached bottom yet. There was 2.32 left on the clock.

The Aggies kicked off and, with a strong front rush, pinned Rice down at the 23. Now the Owls were desperate. Time was fast running out and they were behind by two points. They launched a passing attack. The first pass was intercepted by Pardee, who ran back to the Rice eight. Misfortune multiplied for the Owls when they were penalized five yards down to the three for delaying the game. In a wink, Don Watson knifed over for the third touchdown. It made little difference that the point was missed. The Aggies had scored 20 points in two minutes and eighteen seconds. Now all they had to do was run out the last 1:10 of the clock, which they did.

"It was that onside kick that won for us," said Bryant, the Aggies' coach, afterward. "It was a great kick and that was a wonderful move by Stallings."

*Gene Stallings,
Aggie standout and
present coach (1968)*

*Rice's head coach,
Jess Neely*

The slender, graying Neely, distraught over the sudden turn of the tide, agreed on the shifting point. "We worked like the dickens for 55 minutes and then let the game get away," the Rice coach said. "We knew the onside kick was coming. We called the boys together and talked about it. But we just weren't alert enough."

Dr. David H. Morgan, president of Texas A&M, was one of the first to reach Bryant's side and congratulate him. "I don't believe it, Coach — tell me it's true," he said.

"I don't believe it either," Bryant replied. The Aggies' coach said he had tried to snatch Taylor out of the game after the 55-yard first touchdown because he knew Taylor was tired. "I wanted to put Bobby Conrad in, but I couldn't get him in," Bryant said. "Maybe I was lucky."

Taylor, smiling and lisping through two missing front teeth, said: "It was nothing — all I had to do was run hard."

It took the shell-shocked Owls two years to recover but they reaped their revenge in an emotional, teeth-rattling game in 1957 at Houston. The Aggies were rolling toward another national championship — unbeaten and untied in eight games, only three touchdowns scored against them, ranked No. 1 in the country. The Owls were struggling along with a lackluster 4–3 mark.

You couldn't convince Rice supporters, however, that it was a mismatch. Every inch of space in Rice Stadium was taken up as an SRO crowd of 72,000 poured into the arena. Obviously, there was a thick thirst for vengeance.

The fired-up Rice team, with two fine alternating quarterbacks in Frank Ryan and King Hill, struck quickly. Hill intercepted a pass by the Aggies' Charley Milstead on the Owls' nine-yard line and ran it back to the 21. Then Ryan and Hill took the team 79 yards to the first score. Ryan fumbled on the A&M one-yard line but J. D. Smith recovered for Rice. Hill came in at quarterback and sneaked across for the touchdown. Hill added the extra point that proved decisive.

The frustrated Aggies fought hard to crack Rice's iron resistance but every drive was thrown back short of a touchdown until late in the game. The Aggies got a break when they recovered a fumble on the Rice 15. Roddy Osborne took over for the Aggies. He took the ball on four straight carries, running over for the touchdown from the three. The kick failed and Rice had evened a two-year score, 7–6.

The Owls went on to capture the Conference crown and play Navy in the 1958 Cotton Bowl, losing 20–7.

Bear Bryant's Junction Boys as photographed in 1954

9

The Hurricane Game

OCTOBER 20, 1956

TEXAS A&M	7
TEXAS CHRISTIAN	6

They called them the Junction Boys. They were about as unimposing and lackluster a bunch of ragamuffins as you'd ever hope to see on a college football squad. Yet they become the pride of Coach Paul (Bear) Bryant. Whenever the Bear discussed his teams, in an illustrious career that spanned tenures at Maryland, Kentucky, Texas A&M and Alabama, he always held up his Texas Aggie teams of 1954, 1955 and 1956 as his favorites.

"They weren't much to look at," Bryant, recalling his first look at the team that greeted him in spring practice in 1954. "They weren't actually athletes, most of them. Some were overweight. Others were white-faced. But those that stuck wanted to play ball — and they did. They didn't think anybody in the world could beat them."

They became known as Junction Boys because Bryant's first move in taking over the Texas A&M job was to herd his recruits, almost all of them sophomores, into buses at the College Station campus and take them to a remote spot in the hill country of Junction, Texas, for intensive training. Some of the stories that came back from that camp would peel the skin off your back.

The players were quartered in screened-porch barracks. They were mustered out of their bunks in the early morning like army trainees and were whipped through backbreaking drills almost from morning to night. They skirmished in eye-stinging dust and broiling sun. Coaches were always over them, slapping them on the buttocks and exhorting them to greater effort.

Each day the players would wake up to find another empty bunk, another missing suitcase, another disappearing athlete who had discovered he could not take the grind and so slipped away home. The story is that it took two buses to carry the squad to Junction but only one was needed to bring them back. There were twenty-seven survivors of the ordeal — the hard core of the team that was to rise from the Southwest Conference basement to become champions in three years.

Gene Stallings was one of them, and there was a boy named Lloyd Hale. When five centers quit in one day, Hale, who had never centered a ball in his life, volunteered for the job — and got it. Others were fullback Jack Pardee; Dennis Goehring, who later became an All-America guard; an end, John Tracey; a back, Roddy Osborne; and the explosive John David Crow.

"Every man I had left on the team felt he could whip Joe Louis on Saturday," Bryant said. "The difference between winning and losing is attitude — these boys had attitude."

Nevertheless, the Junction Boys won only one game, losing nine, in their first season, 1954, and finished last in the Conference. The next year they won seven, lost two and tied one.

Then, in 1956, the senior year for most of them, they opened the season by walloping Villanova, 19–0. They edged a powerful Louisiana State team, 9–6; crushed Texas Tech, 40–7, and tied Houston, 14–14. Then, on October 20, they came face-to-face with their key game, opposing a Texas Christian outfit that had Abe Martin as coach and an explosive runner named Jim Swink as spearhead of the offense.

The game was scheduled at College Station. The TCU Horned Frogs, Conference champions the year before with a 9–1 record over-all

Jim Swink of TCU

and ranked fourth nationally, were 14-point favorites. The Frogs had given up only 14 points in mauling Kansas, Texas Tech, Arkansas and Alabama.

Throughout the morning, dark, ugly clouds hovered in the sky and, just at kickoff time, a hurricane blew in, with howling winds and drenching rain. Wind gusts were clocked at 90 to 120 miles an hour. The rain fell in horizontal sheets. But the game went on.

Storms sweeping the bay area near Houston were so bad that twenty-four boats capsized. Two people were killed. Dozens of fishermen were unaccounted for. It was so dark that players couldn't be recognized from the press box. Officials had to hold the ball on the field to prevent it from blowing away.

It was a bizarre setting indeed for a football game, but the players, grimy and wet, sloughed through it. The contest quickly developed into a running battle between TCU's great Jim Swink and A&M's John Crow, with TCU dominating. Shortly after the opening kickoff, TCU, with the wind at its back, splashed through the mud to the A&M two-yard line. On the next play Swink drove into the end zone. But a whistle blast split through the rain and the play was called back. The Horned Frogs were ruled offside. It proved a costly error. TCU lost the ball on downs and A&M, getting nowhere, was forced to punt short of midfield.

The Frogs, behind Swink, smashed downfield again to the Aggies' two. On fourth down, the ball was given to halfback Ken Wineburg, the Conference's rushing leader. Wineburg slashed at the A&M line. When bodies were peeled away, the rain-drenched ball rested on the one. The fierce wind bent the flagpoles to an almost horizontal position and the rain continued to come down in sheets.

A&M's gutty defenders had to kick out of trouble and again braced themselves for another onslaught by the hardest running ballcarriers in the Southwest. By this time the game had moved into the second period. The Horned Frogs, well-named for the stormy occasion, sloughed down the field again and this time moved so close that the tip of the sodden ball almost touched the blotted chalk of the goal line. The official called it fourth down with an inch to go.

A&M sensed that the ball would be given to Swink, and the team braced for it. Sure enough, Swink hit right tackle with a dull thud and it appeared — to all who could see in the eerie darkness — that forward progress had carried him over the goal line. But the man closest to the play — the official — failed to raise his two arms in the traditional sign of a touchdown. The Aggies had the ball again.

The TCU bench erupted in angry protest. Swink, gesturing wildly, insisted he had gone over. His teammates joined in the argument. TCU's Coach Abe Martin rushed in from the sidelines to throw his voice into the dissent. It mattered not. The decision stuck — to be argued by TCU and A&M partisans for years to come — and the violent half ended with no score.

By this time, even in Texas, legends had been built up around the wonder-working powers of Coach Bear Bryant. These legends continued to multiply until, several years later, while turning out national champions at his alma mater, Alabama, there were sacrilegious tales and jokes about the Coach who walked on water.

When the rains and wind abated during the half-time intermission and the sun began playing hide-and-seek with the clouds, one A&M partisan, who had struck it out through the first 30 minutes, was heard to remark, 'The Bear did it. He put in a word Upstairs."

In the third period, with the field still wet but the skies clearing, TCU continued to dominate. Twice the Frogs drove into A&M territory and tried field goals. Vernon Hallbeck missed once from the 15-yard line and another time from the 23. Both kicks were short.

Later in the period, Roddy Osborne, the A&M quarterback, fumbled the ball and a swarm of purple-and-white jerseys fell on the loose oval on the Aggie 29. Jimmy Shofner and Buddy Dike picked up some yardage and then Swink, a nifty runner with good faking moves, started wide to the right, cut sharply and knifed up to the 13. Swink rifled a pass to Shofner in the end zone. Shofner couldn't hold the slippery ball.

By this time TCU partisans were beginning to get edgy again. Were the Frogs going to be stopped another time?

Virgil Miller plunged to the 11. On fourth down, Swink became a decoy as Chuck Curtis faked a handoff, kept the ball, dropped back two steps and shot a pass to O'Day Williams, in the clear on the Aggie goal line. Williams reached up to snare it with one hand, like a baseball outfielder, then fell over the goal. The extra-point attempt failed. But it didn't seem to matter.

TCU 6, Texas A&M 0. It seemed likely to many spectators that the score would stand. However, such reasoners reckoned without the clutch-play proclivities of little Don Watson, a 150-pounder with a reputation for coming through in the big moments; nor did they calculate the determination of the Junction Boys of Bear Bryant.

TCU was hammering away again at the A&M goal line in the fourth period when Chuck Curtis unleashed what appeared to be a sure touchdown pass to Shofner in the end zone. Watson made a tremendous leap and stole the ball from Shofner's hands for an interception and a touchback. The Aggies now had the ball on their own 20. Watson's dramatic and timely interception did not surprise his teammates and the vocal A&M partisans in the hardy crowd of 45,000. He was known as the Aggies' utility man. He could play any position. He could run with the ball, pass and play defense. The year before he had caught a 20-yard pass for one touchdown and had run 51 yards for another in a 19–16 victory that handed TCU its only setback of the year.

The play appeared to inspire the Junction Boys. There was great excitement on the bench. Bryant, his aides and his quarterback held

Roddy Osborne of Texas A&M

*John David Crow holding his Heisman Trophy, which
he received in 1957*

animated strategy sessions. There was still time on the clock to pull out
the game.

On the first play from the Aggie 20, Crow went wide and raced 21
yards to the 41. Then Crow faked a dive and Watson took the ball on
a wing around the left. Before he was brought down, he had rambled
37 yards to the TCU 23. A key block by Ken Beck, knocking out two
TCU tacklers, contributed to the run. Crow picked up three more
yards at guard. The Aggies then went back to wide plays. Crow circled
right end and, with a good block from Watson, moved to the seven.
Osborne picked up two up the middle but on the next play was
smeared for a three-yard loss by end O'Day Williams. The ball was
now on the TCU eight and the Aggies hadn't thrown a pass.

Osborne, faced with a third down play, finally decided to go into
the air for the first time during the game. The Aggies had scored five
of their thirteen touchdowns of the season on passes, so it wasn't that
they lacked an aerial punch. Conditions and circumstances simply
had not dictated a pass. Osborne took the ball and pitched out to Watson. Crow, meanwhile, had sped into the end zone. Watson hit Crow
cleanly with the tying touchdown, 6–6. By this time the sun was
shining brightly and it literally beamed for A&M fans when Loyd
Taylor kicked the ball between the uprights for the extra point. Score:
Texas A&M 7, TCU 6.

Nine minutes were left in the game but the Aggies had no intention now of yielding their slender one-point advantage. They fought like tigers to protect their lead.

It was a bitter pill for the Horned Frogs, now faced with loss of their national ranking and the inside track for a repeat Conference championship. Wineburg, the Conference rushing leader, had been able to gain only 13 yards in eight carries. Swink had done better with 82 yards in twenty-four plays. The Frogs also left the field with the unhappy knowledge that they had wasted six opportunities to score, three of them from inside the two and one from the one-inch line.

It was a tremendous effort for the Junction Boys. Watson, the versatile mite, had triggered the winning touchdown and helped score it. Crow, a brutal runner, had gained 70 yards in nine attempts, Osborne 57 in seventeen. Guard Dennis Goehring was voted the outstanding A&M lineman but top performances also came from guard Murray Trimble, tackle Charles Krusger and end John Tracey. Jack Pardee, Aggie fullback, played with an injured shoulder but contributed thirteen tackles. This was typical of the Aggies' determined, inspired play.

From that Hurricane Day victory, the Aggies rocketed to victories over Baylor, Arkansas, Southern Methodist, Rice and Texas — the latter their first victory in thirty-two years on Austin's Memorial Field — and finished with a record of nine victories, no defeats and a single tie.

As Conference champions, they should have gone to the Cotton Bowl. However, they were faulted for recruiting practices and placed on probation by the National Collegiate Athletic Association.

Their place in the Cotton Bowl was taken by their victim, TCU, which won a memorable game against Syracuse and the great Jimmy Brown, 28–27. This game is described in the next chapter.

Jim Shofner makes a big interception in his own end zone

10

The Heralded Duel Between Jim Swink and Jimmy Brown

COTTON BOWL: JANUARY 1, 1957

TEXAS CHRISTIAN 28
SYRACUSE 27

It was advertised as a personal duel between All-Americans Jimmy Brown of Syracuse and Jim Swink of Texas Christian — and the billings were not exaggerated — but the game was won by an obscure second-string end named Chico Mendoza.

It was Mendoza who rushed in and blocked Brown's attempt for the extra point and thus paved the way for TCU's dramatic 28–27 victory in the Cotton Bowl on January 1, 1957 — the Horned Frogs' first bowl triumph after five post-season setbacks.

The powerful, hard-running Brown fully lived up to his advance notices. He scored 21 points. He hammered out more than half his team's rushing yardage, driving 132 yards in 26 blasts, often carrying Horned Frogs on his back as an automobile might trail bunting. Swink was limited to 41 yards on the ground but he caught a 30-yard pass to set up the winning touchdown, and then he scored it from the three.

Syracuse came to the Cotton Bowl with a vaunted eleven, ranked eighth in the country and best in the East. It was a team typical of those coached by Ben Schwartzwalder, the craggy West Virginian. It was big, strong and versatile, but its emphasis was on straightaway, bone-crushing power football. It was a team superbly drilled in blocking and tackling assignments.

Chief architect of the Eastern team's power game was a 225-pound Negro named Jimmy Brown, son of a prizefighter. Brown himself was built more like a blacksmith, with huge tapering shoulders, arms and legs like pistons and hands the size of young hams. Despite his size, he seemed to glide through openings and, once in full stride, he literally ran over the opposition. In eight Syracuse games, he had scored 106 points and piled up 986 yards.

Swink was smaller but regarded as no less dangerous. Six feet tall, he weighed 185 pounds. He possessed good but not great speed and operated best in the broken field where he specialized in fakes and dazzling cutbacks. During his three-year varsity career, 1954 through 1956, he gained more yards rushing than any back in Southwest Conference history and set a record of twenty touchdowns in one season, 1955. In one game, against Texas in 1955, he piled up 235 yards on the ground.

A rival went to the Bible to describe Swink's running prowess. "Jim giveth a foot as he approacheth a tackler," the player said, "and Jim taketh it away."

Both teams were fired by a desire to atone for past failures. Texas Christian, with a 7–3 record, was in the game on a forfeit, as explained in the preceding chapter. Besides, there was the bitterness of having lost every previous bowl appearance.

Schwartzwalder, whose Christian name was Floyd but who became universally known as Ben, had a bad taste in his mouth, too, which he was anxious to spit out. In the 1952 Orange Bowl game, his Syracuse team had been slaughtered by Alabama 61–6.

There were 68,000 fans in the Cotton Bowl stands that bright New Year's Day, and most of the eyes were on the rival All-Americans, Brown and Swink. They didn't have to wait long for the game to take a quick turn which delighted the highly partisan Texas fans.

Midway in the first period Jimmy Shofner intercepted a running pass by Brown on his own 30. Quarterback Chuck Curtis, who the year before had been carried off the field with broken ribs on the opening kickoff, launched a sharp passing attack that carried the Horned Frogs 70 yards to their first touchdown.

Curtis hit O'Day Williams for 27 yards and Swink for 16 more.

Bobby Dike,
hard runner for the Horned Frogs

TCU's O'Day Williams

Fullback Buddy Dike broke over the middle for 17 and soon there were the Frogs on the Syracuse six. Left end John Nikkel eluded detection of the secondary and Curtis laid a neat pass in his arms in the end zone. Touchdown!

TCU's place-kicker, Harold Pollard, who had missed a conversion in the last Cotton Bowl Game for a 14–13 loss to Mississippi, put the first of his four successful extra points over the bar. The score was 7–0, TCU.

As it developed, Pollard's four extra points provided the final slender margin of victory.

Moments later, Syracuse halfback Ed Ackley was racked up when he took a pitchout going around right end. He fumbled and TCU recovered on the Syracuse 35. The Horned Frogs worked the ball to the eight and on the sixth play of the second period Curtis passed eight yards to Jimmy Shofner for the second TCU score. Syracuse quarterback Fred Kuczala got his arms around Shofner's legs short of the goal line but was unable to hold him. Pollard again converted.

Now the game was more than a quarter old, TCU led 14–0, and people in the stands were whispering, "Where is Jimmy Brown?" They found out soon enough. On the next kickoff, Brown brought the ball

Explosive Jimmy Brown, pursued by end Chico Mendoza (No. 88), tries to turn the corner (Mendoza stops him for a short gain)

back 30 yards to his own 41. Then with an awesome display of ball-carrying — running, like a runaway freight train — he drove 59 yards in seven carries and plunged over from the two for the touchdown. He kicked the point.

A fumble by Dick Finney, TCU's sub quarterback, gave Syracuse possession again on the TCU 24. A pass from Brown to Jimmy Ridlon carried to the four and from there Brown raced around right end for the score. He carried the ball in his right hand and went across without being touched. He again kicked the point, and now the score was 14–14 at the half.

Brown was indirectly responsible for TCU's third touchdown in the third period, the only score of the quarter. Tackled with thunderous force by the tough TCU fullback Bobby Dike, Jimmy coughed up the football and Don Cooper recovered for the Horned Frogs on the TCU

40. Up to this time, the great Swink had been held largely under wraps by the TCU coach, Abe Martin. Knowing that the Orangemen of Syracuse were keying on the clever halfback, Martin had directed Curtis to do a lot of passing.

Now Curtis began mixing up the attack. He threw short, effective passes. He interspersed these with runs by Swink and Dike. The Frogs moved methodically down to the seven. Then, Curtis, rolling to his left and looking for a receiver, noted the Syracuse defense falling back. He trotted the seven yards for the touchdown. Pollard kicked and Texas Christian led 21–14.

It so happened that all of TCU's touchdowns followed Syracuse mistakes — a pass interception and three fumbles. The last occurred early in the fourth period, when the Frogs pounced on another Syracuse fumble on their own 31. With Curtis hitting his targets with pinpoint passing and Swink and Dike picking up hard yardage on the ground, TCU drove to the Syracuse three, and Swink scored. Pollard's fourth conversion gave TCU a 28–14 lead.

On the ensuing kickoff, Brown almost got away. Running hard, ramming through holes and picking up his blocking cleverly, he went 41 yards before he was finally pulled down on the TCU 49. Syracuse pounded away at TCU on the ground, smashing to the four from where Brown plowed over.

It was then that Brown missed his try for the extra point — the play that swung the slender game margin to TCU. Brown's toe was just inches from the ball when Chico Mendoza charged into the Syracuse backfield and leaped sideways. The ball caromed off his left arm. "I had a clear shot in there," the tall substitute end said afterward. It was a vital play.

Syracuse took a TCU punt late in the game on its own 43. Jim Ridlon passed to Dick Lasse for 15 yards in a quick march that moved to the TCU 27. With 1:16 left in the game, Chuck Zimmerman fired a

TCU's head coach, Abe Martin

pass to Ridlon for Syracuse's fourth touchdown. Brown kicked the point, but it was not enough. The Orangemen still were a point behind.

Rather than try for the onside kick, with so short a time remaining, Syracuse chose to kick long and pray for the miracle of a fumble. It didn't happen. TCU ran three line plays and the game was over.

Curtis, the TCU quarterback, was the first to congratulate Brown, who had played one of his greatest games. He had scored three touchdowns, kicked three extra points and rolled up 132 yards on the ground. He far exceeded the rushing performance of his touted rivals, Swink and Dike.

The spearhead of the TCU offense turned out to be Curtis, who completed 12 of 15 passes for 174 yards and two touchdowns, and who scored one touchdown himself.

Buddy Dike, the TCU fullback who was the last man between Brown and the goal line on the fourth period kickoff, praised the Syracuse ballcarrier. "You just can't get a clear shot at him," Dike said. "If you do grab him, he'll carry two or three men with him. He's that strong."

Schwartzwalder agreed that Mendoza was the day's hero. "I saw fullback Alan Cann fussing with our end, Nick Baccile, and I knew we were in trouble," the Syracuse coach said. "Mendoza just slipped past Baccile during the confusion."

Schwartzwalder was asked by reporters if he thought Syracuse's fine but losing effort atoned for the 61–6 defeat he had suffered at Alabama's hands in the Orange Bowl. "No," the coach replied. "When you've lost a game you've lost it. You're out to win a game, not atone for one. We hope to come back someday and do a little better."

Three years later he did. With Ernie Davis performing the deeds of a Jimmy Brown, Syracuse beat Texas in the Cotton Bowl in 1960, 23–14.

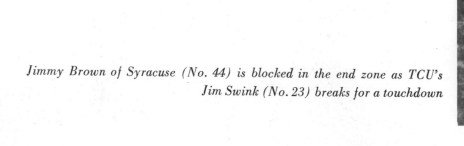

Jimmy Brown of Syracuse (No. 44) is blocked in the end zone as TCU's Jim Swink (No. 23) breaks for a touchdown

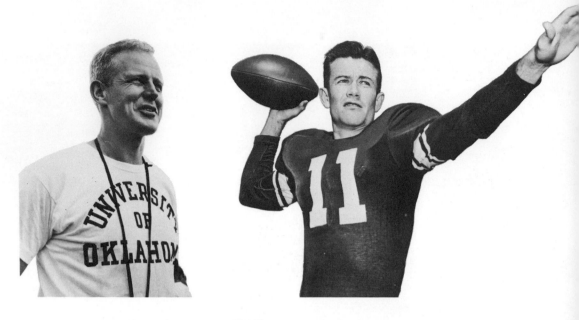

11

Pupil Turns Tables on Teacher

OCTOBER 11, 1958

TEXAS	15
OKLAHOMA	14

After Darrell Royal, in his first year as head coach at the University of Texas, had seen his Longhorns beaten 21–7 by his alma mater, Oklahoma, and his onetime tutor, Charles (Bud) Wilkinson, he was reported to have commented determinedly to a close friend, "That's the last time they'll beat us!"

It is most unlikely that Royal, a mild-mannered, self-effacing man, made such a remark. The story apparently grew out of subsequent events which saw Texas, under the former Wilkinson quarterback, completely turn the tide in the Southwest's most intense and colorful rivalry and run up a phenomenal string of successes against the team he had helped to Conference and national championships.

Wilkinson never again beat his former pupil in their heralded battles of strategy.

The turning point came on October 11, 1958 in Dallas. It was on that day that the United States unleashed its Pioneer rocket shot at the moon — a momentous landmark in the history of science. It was on that day that Royal launched a rocket of his own — a surprise 15–14 triumph over Oklahoma.

Prior to this game, Oklahoma had beaten Texas six times in a row — most of the games by lopsided scores — and nine of the last ten meetings. The Sooners were 13-point favorites in this, the fifty-third time the two Southwest titans had come to grips.

The game, which already had become an early season classic, sent Southwest partisans into orbit and attracted as much national attention as the post-season bowl spectaculars. It carried special appeal because it matched one of the country's foremost coaches against one of his brightest protégés with power-packed teams that eyed No. 1 ranking.

Bud Wilkinson was a handsome, blond graduate of the University of Minnesota with tremendous personal charm and a trigger mind. He became head coach of the Sooners in 1948 and proceeded to amass a record of successes rivaling any the game has known.

After dropping the first game to Santa Clara 20–17, Oklahoma won thirty-one in a row before bowing to Kentucky in the 1951 Sugar Bowl. After losing to Notre Dame in 1952, the team won twenty-nine in a row and took the 1956 Orange Bowl victory to raise the figure to thirty.

Every year from 1948 through 1955, the Sooners won the Big Seven, later the Big Eight, championship. They were named national champions in 1950 and again in 1955. They had perfect season records in 1949, 1950, 1954 and 1955, lost one game in 1948, lost one and tied one in 1952 and again in 1953 and lost two in 1951. They defeated North Carolina in the 1949 Sugar Bowl, Louisiana State in the 1950 Sugar Bowl and Maryland in the Orange Bowl in 1954 and 1956.

In eight years the Sooners lost five games and tied two while winning 73. They won four bowl games and lost one for a combined total of 77 victories, six defeats and two ties. Wilkinson was named Coach of the Year in 1949.

Thus it was an imposing mass of brainpower that young Royal faced on that October afternoon in 1958 — but Wilkinson had taught Royal well.

Royal was cut of the Wilkinson cloth — slender, good-looking in a darker way, quiet, modest and undeniably brilliant. He quarterbacked the great Oklahoma teams of the late 1940s, served as assistant coach at North Carolina State, Tulsa and Mississippi State and head coach at Washington before being lured to Texas by Dana X. Bible.

The key to Royal's coaching philosophy — as that of Wilkinson — was hard work and the development of pride and desire. "A great measure of a coach's success is determined by how well he makes himself understood to his players," Royal once said. "Especially his quarterbacks. I believe this is the strongest quality of Bud Wilkinson. He has a way of expressing himself that leaves no question in a player's mind. By the time a quarterback graduates from Oklahoma, he automatically thinks the way Coach Wilkinson does."

So it was almost a case of two chess masters using the same formula, when young Royal sent his underdog Longhorns against his old teacher for the second time.

The two lean, hard-hitting teams banged away at each other through the early minutes of the game, and Texas mustered the first threat by marching 52 yards to the Oklahoma eight-yard line behind the direction of Vince Matthews, a sub quarterback who had busted a leg during the summer. At this point, the No. 1 quarterback, Bobby Lackey, was rushed into the game. The Longhorns drove to the four and from there Lackey rifled a pass to end Kleo Halm, who, moments before, had snared one good for 30 yards. This time, the ball slipped through Halm's hands and the Texas drive died an agonizing death. The first period ended scoreless.

In the second period, however, Texas struck again with a pair of lightning aerial plays which brought the first touchdown. Originating at his own 48, Lackey stole one of Wilkinson's favorite stratagems — the fullback fake — and hit Reni Ramirez with a pass good for 37 yards. The Longhorns drove to the 10 and then Ramirez changed from the role of receiver to passer and, speeding to the left on a pitch-out, shot a 10-yard pass to George Blanch, who caught it in the pit of his stomach in the end zone. Texas boldly went for the two-point conversion and got it when Don Allen, chugging fullback, crossed from the three. The score 8–0, Texas, and that's the way they went to the half.

A high, short punt by Matthews gave Oklahoma the chance for an equalizer in the third period. Wahoo McDaniel signaled for a fair catch on the Texas 38. Bobby Boyd, a darting dwarf of a quarterback, guided his team to a touchdown in eight plays, halfback Dickie Carpenter sweeping right end for the final five yards. Boyd tried to tie the score with a pass for conversion. He was rushed by Texas jerseys and his throw hit no man's land in the end zone. Score: Texas 8, Oklahoma 6, at the end of the third period.

Early in the last period, the Oklahoma Sooners jarred Texans out of their complacency with a touchdown which came so quickly that many in the stands missed it. Texas had the ball on its own 24. Lackey handed the ball off to Mike Dowdle for a plunge up the middle. Oklahoma's Jerry Thompson hit Dowdle like an army tank, the ball bounding out of his hands before he could gain firm possession. Jim Davis,

Oklahoma's Jim Davis (No. 53) scoring after grabbing a fumble by Mike Dowdle

Vince Matthews of Texas   *Bobby Boyd of Oklahoma*

a larcenous guard, stole the ball and whipped across the goal line in
almost the flick of an eyelash. Lackey was in a position to stop him
but he just stood and stared, goggle-eyed at the suddenness of the
maneuver. Boyd passed to Jerry Tillery for two extra points. Score:
Oklahoma 14, Texas 8. The clock on the scoreboard showed 6:50 left.

It was here that Texas launched its 74-yard winning drive — a thing
of inestimable doggedness and excitement. Matthews, the second-string
quarterback, was at the trigger when Texas started its drive from its
own 26. He began throwing short, effective passes through Oklahoma's
confused secondary defenses. The first was to Bobby Bryant for five,
then to Ramirez for 12. Bryant scooped the ball almost off the grass for
10 more and Matthew hit Blanch with a screen pass for 11.

Thirty-eight yards had been picked up quickly and the partisan crowd
was jumping out of its skin. Wilkinson walked up and down in front
of the Oklahoma bench. Reports from observers in the press box were
sent down to him by telephone and the Oklahoma coach began deploying
defenses in an effort to halt the drive.

It appeared for a moment that these desperate measures might do
the trick. Three plays picked up no yardage and now it was last down

and six on the Oklahoma 36. Matthews sent a pass to Bryant in the left flat. Bryant was hit almost immediately by Sooner end Joe Rector and fullback Prentice Gautt two yards short of the needed yardage. Bryant, with a tremendous second effort, twisted and clawed his way to the 30. Measurement showed it was first down by inches. The Texas goalward march remained alive.

Matthews picked up another 11 yards on a pass to Ramirez and then, changing tactics, sent Mike Dowdle blasting over left tackle for 12. The ball was on the Oklahoma seven with goal to go. At this point, the Oklahoma backbone stiffened and Matthews stalled. A line play gained nothing. The ball was fumbled on a handoff but recovered, again for no yardage. Matthews overshot his mark on a third down pass.

The crowd screamed wildly when Lackey came loping in from the bench. "Old Darrell's got something up his sleeve," commented more than one of the Longhorns' faithful. Lackey took the ball, leaped in the air and shot a quickie pass to Bryant, who was all alone in the end zone. The play caught Oklahoma by complete surprise.

"Lackey is a big, tall boy," Royal explained later. "I wanted somebody who could see over the Oklahoma line. I noticed their middle linebacker was in tight. I was afraid they'd change defense but they didn't."

The touchdown made the score 14–14. Lackey's kick from placement was good for the extra point. Score 15–14, Texas.

With three minutes remaining, Boyd started an Oklahoma rally that carried to the Texas 44. But Lackey had one more great clutch play left in his system. With Boyd trying for a desperate, last-minute pass, Lackey leaped high and made a one-handed interception on the Texas 28.

The gun sounded a moment later. Royal had his victory over his former master and started a series of Texas victories over its archrival that continued for a decade.

"The sagging inhabitants of the big concrete walls couldn't have

Mike Dowdle of Texas

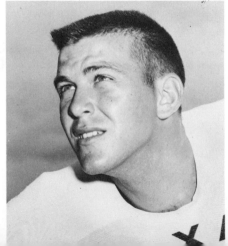
Bob Lackey of Texas

stood much more," wrote sports editor Blackie Sherrod in the Dallas *Times-Herald.*

A cheerleader, Jerry (Red) Herring of Waco, Texas, confided to his Texas mates that the outcome had not surprised him at all. "I live in the same hall with the football team," he said proudly. "I knew we would do it." A short distance away, Cecil Samara, known as Oklahoma's No. 1 booster, was seen splashing orange paint — Texas' colors — on his Model T Ford. He had promised to do it if Texas won. Another Oklahoma supporter, a co-ed, followed suit by painting "Texas" in large orange letters on a 1923 jalopy. "I'm just sick inside," she said.

Lackey confided later that the touchdown pass which won the game had been used only once before during the season — and without success. "I threw it against Tulane," he said. "I had to ground the ball." Bryant, who caught the winning pass, said: "I had been dropping passes all week. When I saw this one coming, I said to myself that I'd better grab it or keep going. I'd never have been able to show my face in Austin."

Wilkinson and Royal met and embraced each other in midfield as fans jumped from the stands and flocked around the players of both teams. "You beat us bad," the Oklahoma coach acknowledged graciously. "You beat us worse than that 15–14 score indicates."

"I thought the game was close," replied Royal, matching his former tutor in graciousness.

There was one ironic twist to the game. The margin of victory came through a two-point conversion, the controversial rule which had only recently been adopted by the colleges as a move to cut down tie games and add last-minute dramatics to the sport. The rule permitted a try for two extra points after a touchdown through a run or a pass instead of the orthodox placement kick for one.

Wilkinson, a member of the rules committee, strongly favored the regulation. Royal opposed it. "I still think it's a good rule," Wilkinson said.

While Lackey emerged as the game's individual star, credit was bestowed on the stouthearted Texas defense, principally tackles James Shillingburg and Dick Jones and ends Bryant and Maurice Doke. Twice they bluned Oklahoma drives of 61 and 51 yards.

"It was a tough but clean game," Wilkinson said. Royal agreed. The limp spectators went home, little concerned about Uncle Sam's historic shot at the moon.

They had had their own pyrotechnics.

12

Texas' Finest Hour

COTTON BOWL: JANUARY 1, 1964

TEXAS 28
NAVY 6

The city of Dallas — Big D, as the natives proudly call it — was tense and jittery. The assassination of President John F. Kennedy at the corner of Elm and Houston Streets only six weeks before hung like a heavy cloud over the entire populace. Although the fatal shots came from the mail-order rifle of Lee Harvey Oswald, many of the people of Dallas felt they had helped press the trigger. There was an unshakable sense of guilt and shame.

The high jinks of another New Year's Eve had not been able to erase it entirely, nor had the prospect now — on this bright, chilly day, January 1, 1964 — of seeing the best college football bowl game in the country, one of the best to come up in years. Host team in the Cotton Bowl was Texas, a hard-striking land force, winner of ten straight games, ranked No. 1 nationally. The invader: No. 2 ranking Navy, with a 9–1 record, 314 points scored and the country's most celebrated individual performer in quarterback Roger Staubach. It was a natural.

Even so, the "Dream Game" was not made without its pressures. Navy barely qualified when Army, inches from the winning goal, let the clock run out in the service classic at Philadelphia, the Midshipmen squeaking through, 21–15. Moments later, in the steamy catacombs of Franklin Field, a telephone rang. Navy received and accepted the bid to the Cotton Bowl.

Reaction was immediate. Some people said it would be disrespectful to the memory of the former President to permit a Navy team to play in the city where the Commander-in-Chief was slain. Protests poured into the Pentagon. Others contended that Kennedy, a PT boat commander in World War II and an avid sports fan, would have wanted the game to be played — if for no other reason than to snap the nation back to life.

Saner heads prevailed. Vice Admiral Charles Kirkpatrick, Superintendent of the Naval Academy, said he had never questioned the advisability of playing. Wayne Hardin, the Navy coach, commented, "It would be in bad taste to associate this game with Kennedy's death."

Overnight, the Navy goat was hijacked. An anonymous caller telephoned the police and said the Cotton Bowl would be blown up if President Johnson's two daughters showed up for the game. A cordon of demolition experts combed the stadium for explosives. Three hundred officers stood watch on the eve of the contest.

By game time, much of the tension had eased, but not entirely. Stanley Marcus of Dallas' big department store, Neiman-Marcus, bought a full-page ad in the Dallas *News,* extolling the merits of the city. Tickets were at a premium. One man offered four seats on the 30-yard line for a job in oil exploration. Another said he'd pay $200 for a pair and throw in an automobile. The game was a 75,504 sellout.

Despite the bomb threat, both Lynda Bird and Lucy Baines, daughters of President Johnson, walked into the stadium about an hour before kickoff. Lynda Bird, 18, a student at the University of Texas, was accompanied by three Secret Service men, one of whom manned a phone. As Lynda Bird took her seat in the student section, newsmen asked her for a prediction of the game.

"I'll leave it to the teams," she said, smiling.

Lucy Baines, also accompanied by Secret Service men, took her place on the opposite side of the stadium. Dressed in a blue suit with white trimmings, she chatted amiably with friends.

Meanwhile, a series of circumstances had fanned the flames of rivalry between the two teams. Navy and its red-hot partisans were convinced that the Midshipmen, with the incomparable quarterback, Roger Staubach, were the best college football team in the country. They still had a bitter taste in their mouths over their single loss of the season — a 32–28 defeat at the hands of Southern Methodist the night of October 11, 1963, in this same Dallas — which undoubtedly knocked them out of the No. 1 ranking. It was a freak game in which SMU went ahead with 2:52 remaining, and Ed (Skip) Orr of Navy bobbled a pass in the end zone as the game-ending gun went off. Navy was determined to atone for this indignity.

Navy supporters in the East ridiculed the national rankings and referred to the Texas Longhorns as a cow country team that shouldn't be allowed on the same field with Staubach and his mates. One sportswriter called the Texans a "hoax and a fraud." He said the players had skinny legs and high rumps like schoolgirls. The Longhorns read these notices and seethed. They attributed the remarks to Navy's Coach Hardin, although Hardin was in no way responsible.

The Longhorns were a little suspicious of Hardin, anyhow. The stocky graduate of California's College of the Pacific had built up a reputation of football chicanery when, in 1959, at the age of thirty-two, he succeeded Eddie Erdelatz. He was accused of using a sleeper against Pittsburgh. Once he sent a second-string quarterback into the game at fullback with a different number to pull a surprise pass play. An acknowledged "gimmick man," he was at his best in cooking up surprises and getting his boys fired up for Army. Once when Army's Coach Paul Dietzel was making a lot of hay with his so-called "Chinese Bandits" defensive platoon, Hardin sent his Midshipmen into the Army–Navy game with Chinese figures on their helmets which said, "Beat Army!" Another time, he had the players' helmets decorated with the pirates' "Jolly Roger" 'emblem — for Roger Staubach.

Roger Staubach, Navy quarterback
and All-American

There was nothing tricky or subtle about Staubach, and Texas knew it. This six-foot-two, 196-pound quarterback from Cincinnati was truly a remarkable athlete. He possessed a rifle arm. He had a rare faculty for spotting receivers and hitting them with radarlike accuracy. He disdained the pocket, rolled out and threw on the run. However, it

Texas quarterback Duke Carlisle (No. 11) passes for a touchdown to wingback Phil Harris (BELOW). Harris hauls in Carlisle's pass over the outstretched hands of Navy Capt. Pat Donnelly

wasn't pinpoint passing alone that made him great. He was even more dangerous when trapped. A scrambler, he had explosive quickness and miraculous balance. It was not uncommon to see him burst from a cluster of enemy tacklers and break into the clear. He ran with long, powerful strides. He had a mysterious knack for direction. He was always dangerous.

Going into the Cotton Bowl game, Staubach had completed 66.4 per cent of his passes (107 of 161) for 1,474 yards and had run for an additional 418 yards. He had figured in fifteen of his team's touchdowns — seven passing and eight rushing. A unanimous All-American choice in his junior year, he had won every major individual award that could go to a player — the Heisman and Maxwell Trophies and the Walter Camp Memorial Trophy, among others. There was no question about it. He threatened to be a handful to an undersized but lightning-quick Texas team which had been primarily a running team throughout the season and had scored only three touchdowns through the air.

The game was virtually a toss-up. Oddsmakers gave Texas a thin one-point edge, principally on its unbeaten record and top national ranking. Betting was heavy on Staubach and the Midshipmen. Their

confidence was high. Hardin, an intent little man with a shock of red hair and piercing blue eyes, appeared more relaxed than usual at the motor inn where Navy was quartered. He chatted amiably with newsmen and removed the curtain from around Staubach, who had been off limits for reporters all season.

Across town, at the Stoneleigh Hotel, Darrell Royal, the young, good-looking coach of Texas, acknowledged that he had the normal pre-game jitters. He had to take a pill to sleep, he said.

Was Royal worried about what Hardin might put on the Navy jerseys? "I worry about what's in those jerseys — not what's on 'em," the Texas coach replied, tersely.

He permitted a leak in his game plans. "For the first time this year, I worked strictly on defense," he said. "Our job will be to keep Staubach from breaking away. When he is allowed to scramble, he can kill you." Asked about his offense, Royal said, "We'll put it right to them."

Tension was high before the game. The Navy band played "Anchors Aweigh." From the Texas side came the strains of "The Eyes of Texas Are Upon You," followed by earsplitting cheers. A Navy Midshipman nudged a mate and said, "Why do they get so excited about 'I've Been Working on the Railroad'?"

Before the kickoff, Blackie Sherrod, sports editor of the Dallas *Times-Herald*, went onto the field to present the "Coach of the Year" Trophy to Royal. The two football teams were standing in the wings, ready to run into the arena. On the side of the field, Hardin was being interviewed by a television announcer with his remarks being transmitted to the crowd over a loudspeaker. "When a challenger plays the champion and wins, he is No. 1!" Hardin's voice beamed through the stands, A loud roar went up from the Navy side.

"We were in line waiting to go out on the field," Phil Harris, Texas wingback, said later. "I was in back. When I looked up the row of Longhorns, I saw every neck grow red."

Hardin, in effect, had said the game would decide the No. 1 ranking in college football, although the honor already had been bestowed on Texas. "I didn't have to give my boys any kind of a pep talk after that — they were ready," Royal said. "Let me put it this way, we weren't a bit afraid to accept the challenge. We were willing to put our No. 1 position on the line."

There was an extra telephone hooked up at the 50-yard line. It was manned by a straight-backed Marine major, Charles Cooper. It went direct to the Chief of Naval Operations, Admiral David L. McDonald, in the Pentagon. The admiral would have been better off if there had been a break in the telephone line.

Ernie Koy of Texas

*Scott Appleton, All-American
tackle for the Longhorns*

The game was only three minutes old when Texas struck for the first touchdown. The ball was on Texas' 42, first down and 10 to go. Duke Carlisle, a spindly-legged, 175-pound Longhorn quarterback, faded back and shot a pass to his wingback, Phil Harris. Harris faked Navy's Pat Donnelly out of position, eluded defender Bob Sutton and went for a touchdown — a play good for 58 yards. Tony Crosby came out in his stocking feet and kicked the point. Texas led, 7–0.

"We were a little lucky," Harris later explained. "Donnelly rotated up to the line of scrimmage and I got behind him. I thought Sutton had me cut off at the sidelines but, when I went back, he lost his balance. It was clear sailing then."

At 9:12 in the second period, the Carlisle-Harris combination struck again, this time on a bomb that covered 63 yards. A Navy punt by Joe Ince rolled dead on the Texas 37. There was a quick huddle, a snap, and Carlisle had the ball in the air again. This time Donnelly almost intercepted but the ball bounced off the Navy defender and into Harris's hands. Texas end, Charles Talbert, screened out the last Navy obstacle and Harris scored standing up.

"I think my elbow hit Donnell's arm," Harris recalled afterward.

"The ball didn't pop out. It just rolled into my hands." Donnelly was distraught later. "I thought I had the ball but I got my feet tangled up and couldn't hold it," he said.

Another Crosby kick and Texas now led, 14–0.

Navy spirits fell. Supporters kept waiting and hoping for the great Staubach suddenly to come alive and save the day, but as the day dragged on it was obvious that Texas had Staubach's number and that the Longhorns' shift to an air game had caught the Midshipmen's defenses completely unprepared.

Staubach hit with his passes, short ones mostly, but every time he started scrambling, he found himself going down under a mass of orange Texas jerseys.

Scott Appleton, Texas' six-three, 240-pound guard was the chief culprit. Time after time, he rushed in to smear Staubach until, by the end of the afternoon, he had accumulated a total of twenty-three tackles, which earned him designation as "Lineman of the Day."

Appleton wasn't alone. Others prominent in stopping Navy's vaunted attack were Tommy Nobis, Dave McWilliams and Knox Nunnally.

Down on the Navy bench, Coach Hardin dug his toe forcefully into the dirt, grabbed the telephone to talk with spies in the press box and

Scott Appleton reaches out to grab Roger Staubach

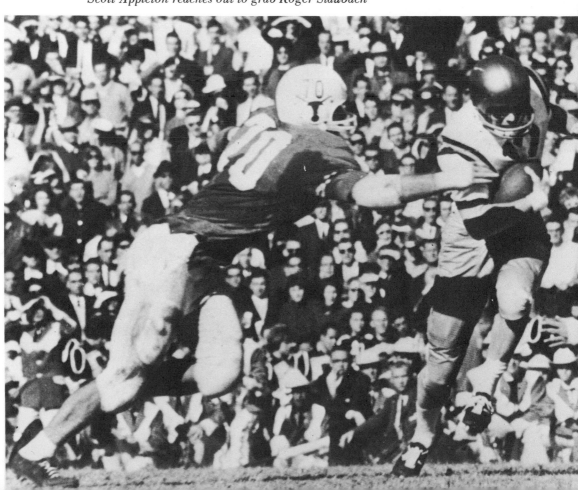

engaged in lively conversations with Staubach. All of it came to no avail.

Texas' skinny-legged boys were fired up and they had Navy well-scouted. Twice Staubach was hit so hard he was jarred loose from the ball. He was thrown for a net loss of 47 yards. Once he was smeared for a 23-yard loss by Knox Nunnally and Pete Lammons. "I've never been hit like that before," Staubach said later. "Every time I looked up, there were a lot of orange jerseys standing over me. I never caught the numerals."

"Toughest rush we saw all year," acknowledged Hardin.

A Staubach fumble set up Texas' third touchdown with 2:30 left in the half. Clayton Lucy hit the Navy signal-caller like a rolling truck and the ball squirted into the hands of Bobby Gamblin on Navy's 34. In seven plays, Texas was across again, Carlisle scoring from the nine. Crosby kicked the point. It was Texas 21–0 at the half.

It was a glassy-eyed bunch of Midshipmen who trooped, dusty and disheartened, to their dressing room at intermission. "It was those two long passes that did it," moaned Donnelly. "If I could have just intercepted one of them, it would have been a different game."

Hardin improvised shifts in both offensive and defensive strategy, instructing Staubach to pass more and run less, but he admitted afterward he knew that it was a hopeless cause. "You just don't hand the nation's No. 1 team a 21–0 lead and beat 'em," the Navy coach told intimates after the game.

In the Texas dressing room, the players were not inclined to celebrate prematurely. They were grim and determined. Ernie Koy, the team's slashing fullback who was on the sidelines in civilian clothes because of a shoulder separation, passed among his teammates, giving each an encouraging slap on the back. Coach Royal talked quietly to Dave McWilliams, the center from Cleburne, Texas, who insisted on playing although his mother had died the previous Saturday. Tommy Ford exhorted his teammates: "Don't let up, gang — we can't let up."

Although the Texas stands rang with the yells, "We're No. 1! We're No. 1!" and the Navy band's "Anchors Aweigh" became less convincing, the last half was anticlimactic. The tone of the game had been set and to every admiral listening all over the world it was obviously now just a question of how bad the defeat.

Texas made it 28–0 in the third period. The Longhorns drove 80 yards in six plays through the reeling, discouraged Navy men, and Harold Phillipp, the sub fullback, plunged over from the two. Crosby kicked his fourth point.

At this stage, Royal pulled out his regulars and threw in his second-

Rival coaches: Wayne Hardin (LEFT) *and Darrell Royal*

and third-stringers, opening the door for a consolation Navy score. Navy took the kickoff late in the third period and launched a 75-yard drive which was climaxed when Staubach sneaked over for a touchdown from the two. One point or two points made no difference but Staubach went gamely for the two-point conversion, failing when the ball slipped through a receiver's hands.

The final score: Texas 28, Navy 6. And Texans felt they could walk straight and tall again.

It was one of the Southwest's most thrilling and most satisfying victories — one which may actually have been won on the drawing board.

"We decided that we must keep Staubach from getting loose," Royal explained afterward. "Throughout the week, we practiced what we called the 'Staubach Shuffle'." We alternated three quarterbacks in the Staubach role, so that they would always be fresh and quick. Then we had our defenders to move in on a line. They were never to let him get outside. They were instructed to keep moving forward and never chase him."

The Navy hero completed 21 of 31 passes for 228 yards, a Cotton

Bowl record, but in twelve carries he was thrown for a net loss of 47 yards. This is how Texas plugged Navy's biggest gun.

Offensively, too, the Longhorns proved more resourceful. Navy was geared to stop Texas' powerful running attack. The Midshipmen threw up a 6–1–4 defense at the start and, at times, had as many as nine men up front. Their plan was to stop Carlisle on option plays and choke off the running of tailback Tommy Ford and fullback Harold Phillipp.

"I couldn't believe it — it looked like a picket fence out there," Royal said. "When I saw that setup, I called Carlisle over and told him to pass." Carlisle had thrown only one touchdown pass all season and Texas as a team had accounted for only two touchdowns through the air. The slender Texas quarterback, whose two long touchdown strikes rocked Navy back on its heels at the start, completed 7 of 19 passes for 213 yards and gained 54 yards on the ground for a new individual offensive record in the Cotton Bowl. His 267 total yards beat by two yards the mark set by Dickie Moegle of Rice ten years before.

Wingback Phil Harris, who had caught five passes all season, brought in three during the game for 157 yards and two touchdowns.

Navy was outfought and outfoxed, and it took its lumps graciously. "Boom! That Texas line really popped us," Hardin commented in the dressing room. "We were never hit like that before."

Vice Admiral Kirkpatrick, Superintendent of the Naval Academy, made a point of going to the Texas dressing room and congratulating Coach Royal. "That was the most beautiful game I ever saw," he said. "There is no doubt who is No. 1."

13
Royal's Gamble That Failed

OCTOBER 17, 1964	
ARKANSAS	**14**
TEXAS	**13**

Paul (Bear) Bryant, the coaching wizard who made his biggest mark at the University of Alabama, is credited with originating the wry remark that a tie is like kissing your sister.

Coach Darrell Royal and his University of Texas Longhorns were in no mood for a sisterly kiss that chill evening of October 17, 1964, when tension hung like a blanket over Austin's Memorial Stadium.

The Texans were fighters, not lovers. It wasn't through sisterly kisses that they were the reigning national college champions, still No. 1 in the rankings and winners of fifteen games in a row.

Now they trailed Arkansas in the titanic battle of unbeaten Southwestern Conference powers, 14–13. The electric clock showed 1:27 remaining. The Longhorns stood within a breath of victory or defeat.

The huge stadium quivered from the impact of the excitement. Every man, woman and child occupying the 65,310 seats in the University of Texas' home field were on their feet, exercising their lungs and straining for a view of the heightening, climactic drama. Others poured down the aisles and surged toward the sidelines, despite the best efforts of the uniformed policemen.

Ernie Koy, Texas' 200-pound tailback, had just smashed over from the one-yard line. This put the Longhorns within a single point of Arkansas's lead.

But Texas wasn't through. It was entitled to try for a conversion and, under college rules, it could attempt a place-kick for one point and tie the game — a near certainty — or it could go for two with a pass or a run. The latter constituted a gamble. What would Darrell Royal, the Texas coach, do?

Marv Kristynik of Texas

Texas called time-out. There were impromptu little conferences at the Texas bench, Royal in the middle of them. Players shuffled on and off the field. Everybody's eye was on David Conway, the Texas place-kicker. He hit fourteen of fourteen from placement during the season. A single point and a tie appeared automatic. But Conway was making no move to enter the game.

The whistle signaled time-in. The orange-shirted Texans went into a huddle and snapped out of it. They lined up in their familiar wing-T formation. The crowd roared. Texas was going for broke.

Quarterback Marvin Kristynik waved to the crowd for silence. He squatted for the snap. He took one step and rolled left. This was a repeat of a reverse pass to the sidelines which Texas had used so effectively in an earlier touchdown drive.

Jim Finch, 195-pound senior Arkansas end, barreled in from the right, got a piece of Kristynik's jersey but couldn't hold him. Finch dropped to the ground, distraught — thinking he had blown it — and started beating his fists into the turf.

Kristynik let the pass fly. But it was a hurried throw and a poor one. It fell short and behind the target, Hix Green, who was wide open crossing the goal line.

In front of the Texas bench, Royal knelt, placed his thumb and forefinger between his eyes and stared into the night. He appeared frozen. Across the field, the Razorbacks grabbed each other and danced in unbounded delight.

A little more than a minute was left in the game. Texas, in desperation, tried an onside kick. Arkansas fell on the ball. Arkansas took no chances. Quarterback Fred Marshall called two snaps, grabbed the ball to his stomach and fell to the ground each time until the gun sounded.

"The greatest victory in Arkansas football history," said the Razorbacks' elated Frank Broyles, who was hoisted onto the shoulders of six of his players and hauled regally off the field.

The slender Arkansas triumph ended a dynasty in the Southwest Conference. It marked the second time in seven years the Razorbacks had been able to beat Texas. Up to that game, Royal had compiled an impressive record of sixty-five overall victories, fifteen defeats and three ties since taking the team's reins in 1957. His Conference record was a gaudy 41–9–2. Texas had either won outright or shared Conference titles four of the last five years. It had gone twenty-five games without a regular-season defeat — the last regular-season setback dating to the next-to-last game of the 1961 campaign when Texas Christian won 6–0. It had played in four bowl games in the last five years. Texas was the reigning national champion.

The Longhorns were 13½-point favorites when the Razorbacks, remembering their bitter 7–3 loss to Texas on the same field two years before, poured into Memorial Stadium that crisp October night. There wasn't a vacant seat in the house.

The two teams were so much alike you couldn't have told them apart had it not been for the different colors of their jerseys. Both were lean and hard. They were not lumbering behemoths whose chief assets were heft and muscle. They had bounce and quickness. They were pursuers. Wherever the ball was, they pounced on it or its possessor in fiery clusters. The main difference lay in the philosophies of the rival coaches. Both Royal and Broyles were stern disciplinarians and perfectionists. They drilled on condition, speed and precision of play execution. But Broyles believed strongly in the pass game — "You've got to be able to throw nowadays," he said — while his rival, Royal, concentrated on ball control. Royal preferred to maintain possession by ripping up consistent yardage on the ground. He usually passed just to keep the other team honest — or in desperation.

Chief operative in Texas' "grind-it-out" style of football was Ernie Koy, who ran with tremendous power. Kristynik, the Longhorns' quarterback, didn't look much like a quarterback. He was five feet ten

Arkansas star Ken Hatfield

inches tall and 170 pounds and he didn't have the moves normally associated with a top-rate field general. But he had one outstanding qualification — he could beat you.

Arkansas's quarterback was Fred Marshall, a six-foot 180-pounder from Memphis who had completed 24 of 39 passes for 321 yards in two spring games. The top ground-gainer was Jack Braeusell, from Van Buren, a relatively small man at 180 pounds and five-nine, but he could spin and turn and run over tacklers head on. Bobby Nix, the fullback, weighed 190. Kenny Hatfield led the nation the year before in punt returns, and he quickly showed Texans why.

After the two teams had battled without score through the first period and 9:24 of the second, Texas' Koy, pinned in his own territory, found it necessary to punt. He got off a good, arching, spiraling boot that wafted into the arms of Hatfield, standing on his own 19. With a wave of orange jerseys sweeping down on him, Hatfield retreated a couple of steps, avoided one tackler, let another spin by and then picked up his own blockers. He found an alley down the left sideline, past Arkansas's bench, and he rambled 81 yards to a touchdown.

"The greatest blocking I've ever seen," Hatfield modestly said later. "No one touched me — not a hand — once I got to the wall."

Tom McKnelly kicked the extra point and Arkansas led 7–0.

Both Royal and Broyles admitted that the spectacular run set the tone for the game. It stiffened the backbone and buoyed the confidence of the underdog Razorbacks. It rocked the all-winning Longhorns back on their cleated heels. "It didn't surprise me," Royal said later. "This boy had been doing it for them for three years. You let up a minute and you're in trouble. They gave him great blocking."

"In a game between two closely-matched teams, something like this can give a team a little extra," Broyles said. "It put more spark in our kids. They were more determined to win."

The third period was scoreless. The top-ranked Texans hawked the ball and hit with such fury that the Razorbacks were held to a single first down. It appeared only a matter of time before the powerful Longhorns would wrest the game from their guests, as expected.

Early in the fourth period, Koy, slamming away at the Arkansas defenses, led a 46-yard drive that gave the Longhorns the matching touchdown. Phil Harris scored it from the two and Conway kicked the point to make it 7–7.

It was after this touchdown that Texas got a bad break that probably, in the final analysis, cost it the game. Arkansas, fourth down and deep in its own territory, was forced to punt. The ball was snapped quickly

Longhorn Phil Harris

125

and the kick soared down the field, taken by Texas on its own 40. Then a flag dropped. Texas was penalized for having twelve men on the field. In changing platoons, one man didn't get to the bench in time.

Instead of having the ball on their own 40 — "with momentum," as Royal put it — Arkansas retained possession and went on to what ultimately proved the winning touchdown.

Later, Royal took the reverse break philosophically. "What a way to let them keep a drive going," he said. "I'll take the blame for it. It was poor coaching. We worked hard on getting the men on and off the field but they were just too fast with the snap. It was a smart play on their part. I think it was the crucial play of the ball game."

The Razorbacks went 70 yards to the touchdown. The drive was climaxed by another dramatic stroke — a 34-yard pass from Marshall to end Bobby Crockett, who caught the ball in full flight between a pair of Texas defenders and raced into the end zone. McKnelly again kicked the point. Score: Arkansas 14, Texas 7. Time left: 6:43.

Crockett, who made the vital catch, was a substitute for Jerry Lamb, who had been injured in the first period and never returned. "It was a perfect pass," Crockett said, "but I thought it would never come down."

Texas still had some gristle left. Taking the kickoff on its own 3, the smarting Longhorns started plugging away toward the Arkansas goal. The ground came in small, hard-earned spurts but it was enough for the first downs, to throw a little panic into the Razorbacks and raise the spirits of the wild, pro-Texas crowd.

Koy was the chief gainer but there was an occasional sweep or short pass by Krystynik and a plunge by Hix Green. Minutes ticked away rapidly and the clock showed 2:10 left when the Longhorns moved up to the Arkansas 12-yard line, now definitely within striking distance.

With Koy getting some rest and some strategy tips on the sidelines,

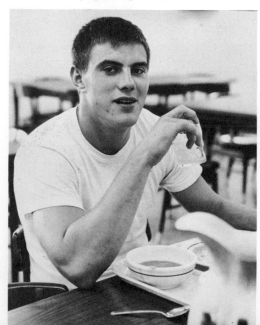

Bobby Crockett of Arkansas

126

Green gained four on a straight-ahead dive play. Kristynik sent Green wide on a sweep but linebacker Ron Caveness of the Razorbacks tore in and forced the play out-of-bounds for a four-yard loss.

A loud cheer went up when Koy returned to the game. Tension heightened. Arkansas tackle Jim Williams broke through and downed Koy, attempting to pass, on the 17. Arkansas supporters breathed easier. It was now fourth down and 15 yards to go, and time was escaping fast.

Then came a break for Texas. An Arkansas player was seen grabbing a face mask — a penalty. Arkansas was penalized half the distance to the goal and Texas got the ball on the Arkansas 8½-yard line. On the next play, fullback Harold Phillipp shot through a hole and drove to the one. With first down and goal to go, Kristynik faked to Phillipp, handed off to Koy on an inside belly series trap play and watched Koy slide across for the touchdown.

Then came the decision — should Texas go for the tie or the victory?

"It was a bench call," the quarterback, Kristynik, said afterward. There was never any doubt in my mind or in the mind of Coach Royal. We had to have a win — or nothing."

"We never considered a kick," acknowledged Royal. "The only problem in my mind was whether we should ram it at them or go for a pass. I knew they'd be looking for a pass. But those are three long yards to run for. I made the decision — I'll take the blame."

"It was a good play," Kristynik said. "It was a tailback flare, a fake run and a pass. Hix had caught it for us on our touchdown drive, good for seven yards. We felt sure we could complete it again. When I took the snap, I wheeled and it looked like someone was right there on me. Hix was open for just a second there, but I hurried my throw."

Green was distraught that he couldn't get to the ball, but it was impossible. "Marvin couldn't get it to me like he wanted to," he said. "It got to me on a bounce."

It could have been by divine decree.

Two years before, Texas had beaten Arkansas 7–3, scoring in the last thirty-six seconds of the game to hand the Razorbacks their only setback of the season.

In that game — as in this one — was Jerry Welch, 212-pound Arkansas guard.

"When they lined up for that conversion, I mumbled to myself, 'Please, Lord, don't let it happen again.' I think He heard me."

Anderson cuts to full stride for a 13-yard gain

14

"Throw It to Me,"
Anderson Said

OCTOBER 2, 1965

TEXAS TECH   20
TEXAS A&M   16

It was a desperate situation for the Red Raiders of Texas Tech. The score was 16–13 in favor of Texas A&M. The clock on the scoreboard that Saturday evening, October 2, 1965, in Texas Tech's Jones Stadium at Lubbock showed the seconds ticking away with only 1:38 left in the ball game.

The Raiders were at the Aggies' 49, a spot which television broadcasters might charitably term "good field position," but it was third down and 10 yards to go. If the Raiders failed here, the odds were that the Aggies would regain possession and hold the ball until time ran out.

Besides, the Aggies had given ground grudgingly. The Raiders were behind 10–0 at the half and they had been plodding uphill most of the game.

As the Raiders went into the huddle, a substitute ran in from the bench with a play from Coach J. T. King.

"Coach wants you to use Number Seventy," the messenger said.

This was a sideline hook pass which quarterback Tom Wilson had worked effectively with rangy, 187-pound end Jerry Shipley, but a play which the Aggies almost certainly would be looking for.

"Okay, Number Seventy," barked Wilson. "You guys know what to do. Get out there, Jerry. Let's go."

"I'll be right behind you," halfback Donny Anderson said to Shipley. "If you get into trouble, give it to me. I think I can make it."

There was a snap. Wilson faded back. Shipley, from the split left end position, ran the hook pattern, raced seven yards downfield, spun and was waiting at the 42 when the ball sped into his arms.

Anderson, the strapping six-foot-three halfback — who was destined to win All-America honors and then sign a near half-millon-dollar contract with the pro Green Bay Packers — was at his appointed place.

Slotted to the right, Anderson was bumped hard by Aggie tackle John Nilson as he crossed the scrimmage line and the Aggies' Monster Man, Ken Caffey, cut across the Raider halfback's path.

Caffey hit Shipley with rattling impact a split second after Shipley lateraled the ball to Anderson. The suckered Aggies' defense poured in on Shipley as Anderson took the ball and had almost clear sailing to the goal line.

"I knew nobody was going to catch me once I got the ball," Anderson said later.

After crossing the goal line, he threw the ball against the ground. Then he sat down and cried unashamedly.

"I believe it's the first time I ever cried like that," the Raider halfback confessed afterward. "I couldn't help it."

The improvised 40-yard play gave Texas Tech a 20–16 victory. Many observers said it was on that night that the Raiders came of age in the Southwest Conference.

"This could be the greatest thing that ever happened to Texas Tech in Southwest Conference football," said Coach King.

Texas Tech was a latecomer to Southwest football. It fielded its first varsity team in 1925. It played for years in the Border Conference, dominating the football races, while seeking entry in the Southwest Conference. Finally, in 1956 it was formally admitted, but it was not until 1960 that it was able to schedule enough teams in the Conference to qualify as a football member.

Harry Ledbetter,
the Aggies' quarterback

Going was slow at first. The Raiders finished in a tie for sixth in the eight-team league in 1960, 1961 and 1963, was last in 1962 and rose to fifth in 1964. In the middle 1960s, with the impetus provided by Donny Anderson and other players of similar stature, the men from Lubbock established themselves as a definite factor in the Southwest Conference. By the late 1960s, they were in the thick of the title scramble.

Perhaps more than anyone else, it was Anderson who put Texas Tech on the national football map.

He was the classic picture of the college football hero, a Golden Boy with many of the characteristics of Paul Hornung, whose place he took with the National Football League Packers. Six-three, 205 pounds, he was lean and strong with deceptive speed.

His bulldog head, topped by close-cropped blond hair, sat close on wide, tapering shoulders. He appeared to have no waist. His muscle-bulging legs moved like those of a thoroughbred racehorse. He ran the 100 in ten seconds flat but he was quick on the getaway — he had what auto buffs call torque. He took much pride in the fact he could spurt twenty yards in :02.5 and forty yards in :04.5. He also was an ace pass receiver and punter.

Joe Jones, a Baylor defensive back, said of him, "Usually you can block a guy down, but not Anderson. You've got to lock both arms around his knees, hang on and hope." Another opponent, Frank Horack, Texas Christian defensive back, said, "You can't relax when Anderson has the ball. We stopped him off tackle one play cold, but he spun off. He just turned the corner and went 90 yards for a touchdown."

With Anderson playing his senior year and with a well-balanced team to back him up, Texas Tech had high hopes for the 1965 season.

A standing-room-only crowd of forty-three thousand jammed into Lubbock's Jones Stadium for the Tech-Aggie game. It was the Conference debut of the Aggies' new young coach, Gene Stallings, who had played for Coach Paul (Bear) Bryant at Texas A&M. Fans anticipated a lot of action from the rival quarterbacks, Wilson of Texas Tech and Harry Ledbetter of Texas A&M.

The Aggies got off to a quick start. Midway in the opening period A&M's middle guard, Tom Murrah, pounced on a ball that had slipped from Wilson's hands, and it was the Aggies in possession on Tech's 43. Ledbetter swung into action. He moved his team down to the 20 only to have his team pushed back to the 35 by a holding penalty. Then he completed a 14-yard pass to Dude McLean to almost wipe out the penalty loss. Dan Schneider bulled for three. Bill Sallee weaved his way for six more, and Ledbetter, on a keep, made it first down on the 10. A personal foul penalty against Tech moved the ball to the five. Ledbetter ran twice and then threw an in-motion pass to Lloyd Curington. Curington grabbed the ball at the hash marks and scored with 2:39 left in the opening period.

It was a three-yard touchdown pass. Glynn Lindsey, A&M's place-kick specialist, converted and the Aggies led, 7–0.

Moments later, early in the second period, the Aggies were on the move again, driving 68 yards to Tech's one-yard line. Tech stiffened and held. On A&M's final try, the ball was given to Curington. Dennis Tucker and Guy Griffis of the Raiders crashed through to throw Curington for a one-yard loss.

After an exchange of punts, the Aggies, dominating the opening half, again drove deep into Tech territory, only to be stopped again at the five. This time the Aggies elected to try for a field goal and Lindsey sent the ball through the uprights from 22 yards out.

Texas A&M led, 10–0, and that was the score they carried during intermission.

Texas Tech's offense had sputtered and fizzled through the first half of the game. The Aggies had assigned Ken Caffey to the Raiders' running ace, Anderson. Caffey was known as the Monster, not because of his size — only 191 pounds — but because of his quickness and

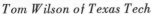

Tom Wilson of Texas Tech

*Ken Caffey, who was on
Anderson man to man*

toughness. As a result, Donny was held in a virtual straitjacket. Wilson was rushed so hard that he was able to pass for only 57 yards.

During the half-time intermission, Tech's disappointed coach, J. T. King, didn't chew out his athletes, as is sometimes the custom. He showed them movies.

These were playbacks of video tapes of the game taken by two assistant coaches — one concentrating on defense and the other on offense. The $25,000 machine had been loaned to Tech by a businessman and friend of the school. It marked the first use of such electronic equipment in college football.

"We were able to see exactly what the Aggies were doing," King explained later. "For one thing, we learned that A&M's Ken Caffey was playing Anderson man-to-man, so we keyed off Donny for a while to stop this. We saw that when we ran a rollout sideline pass, Aggie defenders were going with the receiver and leaving the quarterback free. So Wilson was ordered to fake sideline passes and run with the ball. Also, one reason that we didn't move the ball well in the opening half was that we were trying to run too many plays. In the second half, we reduced our repertoire to five passing plays and four running plays. It proved very effective."

It was a different Tech that played the second half. Late in the third period, Guy Griffis, 180-pound Tech halfback, returned an A&M punt from his own 46 to the Aggie 39. Penalties cost the Raiders heavily and soon they found themselves back on the 49 with third down and 20 yards to go for a first down.

Wilson tossed a beautiful 38-yard pass to Shipley, who faked defender Eddie McKaughan out of position and snuggled the ball to his chest at the 11. Johnny Agan picked up a yard, and Mike Leinert smashed to the eight. Ground was coming dearly. On third down, Wilson rifled a pass to Anderson, who literally tore himself from Robert Cortez's grasp and barrelled across for Tech's first score.

Bob Bearden kicked the point and the Aggies' lead had been cut to an uncomfortable 10–7.

The two teams fought like wildcats through the remainder of the third period and through most of the fourth, setting the stage for the gripping climax which saw three touchdowns scored in the final 2:44 and the lead change hands as many times.

During the scoreless period of about twenty minutes, bridging the last two quarters, the revived Tech Raiders drove once to A&M's 23-yard line and another time to the 32, only to stall. Once they tried a 47-yard field goal but the kick by Roger Gill hit the crossbar and bounced back. It was that kind of a night.

Tech went ahead late in the fourth period, traveling 59 yards on twelve plays principally on the passing of Wilson and the running of Leinert, Shipley and Anderson. During that drive, Anderson made a leaping one-handed catch of a Wilson pass, good for 21 yards and a

Tech's Jerry Shipley

Halfback Mike Leinert of Texas Tech

first down at the Aggies' 28. Then, noting that the Aggie defenders were refusing to blitz but were falling back to guard receivers, Wilson kept the ball and sped 14 yards.

From there the Raiders moved to the Aggies' one, where Texas A&M stiffened its resistance. With fourth down and inches to go, Wilson faked beautifully and flipped to Leinert wide at the right. Leinert, a sophomore somersaulted over Aggie linebacker Joe Wellborn into the end zone.

It seemed immaterial at the time that Bearden's try for placement went wide. Tech led for the first time, 13–10, and the clock showed 2:44 remaining. Raider followers became delirious but they soon were brought back to earth.

The Aggies took the next kickoff and in four plays — two incomplete passes and two that went for bombs — covered 79 yards for the touchdown that put them back in front.

The 195-pound Ledbetter was at the throttle. His first pass, aimed at Dude McLean, missed. On the next play, the Aggie quarterback arched a long pass to McLean who battled Tech defender Robert Yancer for the ball and won. The two fell on the Tech 40 — a 39-yard gain.

The seconds ticked away as Ledbetter tried for his favorite target — McLean — again. The ball sailed over McLean's head. Then Ledbetter

Donny Anderson

shot a long, arching pass to Jim Stabler, who had managed to speed past the Tech secondary. Stabler grabbed the ball on the six and ambled across the goal line.

The kick failed, but the Aggies led 16–13. It looked like another heartbreaker for the Raiders.

The clock showed only 1:38 remaining when Kenny Baker took the short kickoff and brought the ball back to the Aggies' 49. The Aggies had gambled on keeping possession with an onside kick. The gamble failed.

Wilson's first pass overshot Anderson. His second, a wide one to Leinert, saw the maneuver smothered at the line of scrimmage.

Then came the dramatic third-down play from the bench and Anderson's improvisation in the huddle: "Let me have it."

When Anderson scored the winning touchdown with little more than a minute remaining, pandemonium broke out in the stands. On the Raider bench, a solemn Tech defensive player, Guy Griffis, broke into the broadest grin of all.

It was Griffis who had been faked out of position a few moments before on the long pass to Stabler which had sent the Aggies into the lead and which, at the time, appeared to have sewn up the game for A&M. After yielding the touchdown, Griffis had been yanked and he was suffering inner torture on the sidelines when the sudden break occurred.

"If we hadn't won, I'd have surely been the goat of this game," Griffis said. "I don't know what happened on that Stabler pass. I didn't see Stabler at all. I watched their end come down and break across. I took off after him. Then suddenly I saw Ledbetter set. I knew then that there was a man down there, and that he was alone. It was an awful sickening feeling."

Coach King of the Raiders generously passed around credit for the victory. "It was marvelous the way the boys cooked up that winning play in the huddle," he said. "Anderson deserves a world of credit. But I must also give credit to the defense. If our defense hadn't stopped them on the one-yard line in the first half, they would have gone to intermission with a 17–0 lead. I doubt that we could have overcome that. The video tapes were a tremendous help. They changed us from an ineffective, bumbling team to a winning team."

Stallings, the young A&M coach, shouldered the blame for permitting the game-winning strike.

"I didn't have them ready for a play like that," he said. "It was poor coaching."

No excuses were necessary on either side. It was a game that could

Texas Tech's head coach, J. T. King

have gone either way. It was a game that lived up to the tradition of the Southwest.

Wilson, who went into the game suffering with a sore back, connected on 18 of 30 passes for 238 yards and three touchdowns. The Aggies managed to stop Anderson on the ground, limiting him to 21 yards in fifteen carries for an average of 1.4, but it was All-American Donny who hurt them most with his pass receptions.

The Aggies' Ledbetter had 13 hits in 25 passes for 190 yards. His favorite target was Dude McLean, who made six catches for 95 yards. Each team was limited to 79 yards on the ground.

The Raiders lost only one other game, the final game with Arkansas 42–24 and went on to the Gator Bowl in Jacksonville, Florida, where they bowed to Georgia Tech 31–21 despite a fine performance by Anderson.

Later Anderson, who reportedly was offered a $50,000 mansion and a contract of well over half a million dollars by Houston of the rival American Football League, cast his lot with the National Football League Green Bay Packers.

The blond, good-looking Anderson signed the pro contract in a Hollywood setting at Jacksonville and went on to bigger things.

15

Arkansas' Encore Is Even Better

OCTOBER 16, 1965

ARKANSAS	**27**
TEXAS	**24**

Marvelous Marvin Kristynik was in a dither.

"My contact lenses," the University of Texas quarterback said to a teammate. "I don't have any contact lenses. I'm sure I left them in the motel room back in Fort Smith."

It was now 11 A.M. In a couple of hours, the Texas football team would be taking the field against Arkansas in college football's Game of the Day — later to be labeled the Game of the Era — and there was Texas' No. 1 signal-caller and passing ace unable to see the stadium without his glasses.

The Texas football team, because of the scarcity of rooms, had been forced to spend the night at Fort Smith, sixty miles from Fayetteville, home of the Razorbacks and the site of the game which was sure to determine the top-ranking team in the country. Both had 4–0 records. Texas was No. 1, Arkansas No. 3.

Near panic, Kristynik was reluctant to tell head coach Darrell Royal of his stupidity. Instead, he went to one of the assistant coaches. A prominent Texas alumnus, Jack Perry of Houston, came to the rescue. He had a small private jet plane parked at the airport. The Fayetteville police provided a motorcycle escort to the airport, sirens screaming. In less than an hour, Perry was back with the lenses. They had been found, luckily, in the lavatory at the motel where the Longhorn team had been quartered.

Royal wasn't told of the incident until later. It was probably just as well. As it turned out, he had enough excitement and frustration in one day to last an ordinary human a year.

If Southwest Conference football fans wondered what they could ever get as a proper encore to the pulse-pounding climax of the 1964 Arkansas–Texas game (described in Chapter 13), they had to wait only twelve months for the answer.

The game had all the ingredients. Texas had won 25 of its last 26 regular season games. Arkansas was in the throes of a sixteen-game winning streak, longest in the country, but this year neither team had been properly tested. In sweeping past its first four opponents, Arkansas rolled up 114 points to 33 for its rivals. The Longhorns' point spread was even better — 110–19.

Although the game was being played on Arkansas' home field — Razorback Stadium, with a capacity of only 39,700 — and although the Razorbacks had won the year before in Austin, Texas was a seven-point favorite. The contest was chosen for national television.

To the overflow forty-two thousand who crammed into the cozy stadium and to the millions who watched on television, the battle produced the kind of drama that Hollywood scenario writers would scoff at as being too unreal for belief. Arkansas got off to an astonishing 20–0 lead. Texas bounded back to go in front 24–20. Then Arkansas pulled out the victory in the final two minutes with a spectacular air strike. A couple of years afterward, Southwest Conference sports writers and broadcasters, asked to vote on the ten best games of all time in the section, unhesitatingly named this game No. 2, beaten out only by the 1949 heartstopper between Notre Dame and Southern Methodist.

Fans take their football seriously in the Southwest, but nowhere does the game generate greater fervor than in Arkansas.

Razorback faithful began looking toward the big collision with Texas weeks in advance. They bought red hats, red vests, red coats and red dresses (Arkansas colors are cardinal and white). They painted signs and hung them everywhere. They composed folk songs about their favorite players and these were heard constantly on the radio, in barbershops and on the streets.

One of the favorite folk songs featured Jon Brittenum, the team's star quarterback. Set to the tune of "John Henry," it went something like this:

> *When Jon Brittenum was a little bitty boy,*
> *Sittin' on his mammy's knee.*
> *Well, he said to his mother, don't you worry now,*
> *Big Frank'll make a quarterback o' me,*
> *Big Frank'll make a quarterback o' me.*

They sang it from the Ozark Hills to the Mississippi River bottoms —

Jim Brittenum, Arkansas's star quarterback

from Poplar Bluff to Terrapin Neck — and as the big game neared, amateur lyricists added their own verses. Another went like this:

> *Well, Jon, he said to the coaches,*
> *Let me toss the pigskin around,*
> *If I call the signals for your Razorback team,*
> *I know I'll do the best I can . . .*
> *You know I'll do the best I can.*

Brittenum was Coach Frank Broyles's chief weapon, although Arkansas was gifted with a vicious and dangerous ballcarrier in Harry Jones, a speedy and sure-fingered split end in Bobby Crockett and a squad of exceptional speed and toughness.

Brittenum was a six-foot, 180-pounder from Brinkley, Arkansas, who entered the university in 1962, lettered as a sophomore in 1963 but remained out of action in 1964 when he was "red-shirted" so he would be available for the 1965 and 1966 seasons. He was a quick rollout passer with an excellent arm. In his first complete year, he hit on 75 of 149 passes for 1,103 yards and eight touchdowns. He scored six touch-

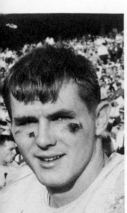

*Harry Jones
of Arkansas*

downs on the ground. In the 1964 Cotton Bowl, he completed 15 of 24 passes for 177 yards. So his statistics deserved being set to music.

Harry Jones, from Enid, Oklahoma, was a fleet, long-legged breakaway runner, Six-feet-two, 195 pounds, he was Arkansas's main ball-carrying threat. Texas realized that if it concentrated on Jones, Brittenum would pass; if it concentrated on Brittenum, Jones would run. It was not a bright prospect.

While official oddsmakers made Texas the favorite, everybody in Arkansas was convinced that the Razorbacks would win, and they didn't mind showing it.

Fayetteville was festooned with banners. They hung over banks, restaurants, business houses and even churches. "Go, Hogs, Go. Beat Texas. Fryers 29 Cents a Pound." That was typical. Motel marquees said: "No vacancy. Beat Texas." The billboard in front of Fayetteville's First Baptist Church had this quieting message: "Football is only a game. Eternal things are spiritual. Nevertheless, Beat Texas."

Perhaps it was an overdose of this sort of hometown exuberance and confidence that affected Texas' Coach Darrell Royal, who appeared unusually grim when he walked onto the field prior to the game. A reporter, noticing the Texas coach's glumness, reminded Royal, in half-jest, that he appeared very serious while Frank Broyles, the Arkansas head coach, was relaxed and smiling. "If anybody's smiling on an occasion like this," Royal replied tartly, "it's because he's nervous."

If Royal was tense and nervous before the game started, he must have felt an anvil in his stomach moments after the game got under way. The fans had hardly settled in their seats when Brittenum hit on a 58-yard touchdown pass, only to have it nullified by a penalty. Moments later, Bobby Nix of Arkansas, the 198-pound fullback and punting specialist, kicked to Texas' Phil Harris, who tried to handle the ball inside the five-yard line. Jim Williams, a 205-pound Razorback tackle, hit Harris like a thunderbolt. The ball bounded into the end zone and Maryine Bercher, an Arkansas halfback, pounced on it for a touchdown. Ronnie South kicked the extra point. Arkansas led, 7–0.

"I misjudged the ball," Harris explained afterward. "I thought it was going to bounce into the end zone, but it bounced straight up. I grabbed it. I don't know who hit me, but he really creamed me."

The Longhorns bounded back and, behind Kristynik's expert direction, marched to the Arkansas 20. There Harris became the victim of another tough break. He bobbled a handoff, and Tommy Trantham, a towering defensive end for the Razorbacks, grabbed the ball in midair and, deftly picking up a cordon of blockers, raced 77 yards to a second

Razorback touchdown. Ronnie South's try for extra point was blocked. The score: Arkansas 13, Texas 0. It was still the first quarter.

"Trantham just grabbed my arm and the ball plopped out," an embarrassed Harris explained.

By this time the Longhorns were reeling and the Razorbacks were rolling — their confidence soaring and their momentum strong. Early in the second quarter, the Razorbacks got their third touchdown by working for it. No quick breaks this time but simply hard-hitting football — 60 yards in nine plays. Bobby Burnett pounded away at the middle of Texas' line. Brittenum passed 23 yards to Harry Jones at the Texas 15. Two plays later, Brittenum passed 11 yards to Bobby Crockett for a touchdown. South converted. The game was 18:57 old and Arkansas led 20–0. "Whoooo, pig, sooey!" echoed and reechoed through the happy Arkansas stands.

Tommy Trantham of Arkansas on his way to a touchdown after
Phil Harris had fumbled

Any celebration, however, was premature. After all, Texas was the No. 1 college team in the country. It could hit and it could hurt. The Longhorns managed to score 10 points before the half. Kristynik, his vision 20-20 with the recovered contact lenses, passed the team into position for a 35-yard field goal by Dave Conway. Then he threw a 42-yard pass to Les Derrick which put Texas in scoring position. Kristynik obliged by going over from the one.

Coach Darrell Royal is not a locker-room orator of the Knute Rockne stripe. But they say he can be firm and, with a few well-chosen words, can turn a whipped and whimpering cat into a ferocious beast. The Texas players came out of the locker room for the second half, fired-up and eager enough to jump out of their moleskins.

The Longhorns weren't long in asserting themselves. They launched a third-quarter drive but stalled at the 34 and allowed Conway to kick another field goal. Now they had momentum. They took a short kick on the Arkansas 40 and Kristynik moved them to a touchdown in seven plays, scoring himself on a 14-yard sweep. There was a second successful conversion and Arkansas' early lead had disappeared, 21–20. Texas had not spent its load. Kristynik got the Longhorns moving again and Conway kicked his third field goal, from 34 yards, to send Texas ahead, 24–20, with only minutes remaining in the game. Arkansas now needed a touchdown to win. Many a red hat in the stands was pulled low over the eyes in despair.

Brittenum quickly brought Arkansas supporters back to life. With the ball on his own 20, he hit Bobby Crockett with a 22-yard pass that pushed up to the 42. Linebacker Tommy Nobis, Texas' rugged All-America star, was the man who brought down the Razorback end.

The clock showed 3:20 to play. Texas began blitzing Brittenum and Coach Broyles countered by sending in Jim Lindsey, a wingback who had spent most of the day on the bench watching junior Harry Jones carry out his assignments. Lindsey ripped up to midfield.

Brittenum, rolling out, began hitting Crocket for short gains which Texasc seemed unable to stop. Ten yards . . . eight . . . ten more. Arkansas was on Texas' 22. The crowd now was hysterical.

Crockett was spinning and turning and catching. The Longhorns put two men on him. Arkansas completed a pass to Bobby Burnett at the 15. The Razorbacks called time-out. The clock showed 1:44 remaining. Crocket was called to the bench for a brief respite. The Razorbacks sent in Martine Bercher, who raced up the middle and almost scored on a diving catch in the end zone, but the ball tipped out of his fingers.

It was third down and four at the 15 when Crockett raced back onto the field amid deafening cheers. Arkansas pulled the same play. Brit-

Tommy Nobis,
all-time linebacker
from Texas

tenum rolled to the right and Crockett angled toward the right corner by the flag. Crockett, delayed illegally at the line of scrimmage by Texas end Barney Giles, slipped past Giles and caught the pass on his fingertips. The pass was good for 14-plus yards, as Crockett tumbled out-of-bounds inches from the goal line.

There was momentary suspense when an official's flag went down. But the penalty was against Texas — Giles's infraction against Crockett at the scrimmage line — and the penalty was refused.

Brittenum took the ball the remaining inches on a quarterback sneak. South kicked the point and that was the ball game: Arkansas 27, Texas 24.

"Crockett told me before that last drive that if I got the ball to him a little higher, he'd have a better chance of catching it," Brittenum said afterward. "I saw him go down but I was afraid he wouldn't turn around. I yelled 'Crockett!' and then I threw it, leading him as much as I could."

Bobby Crockett is mobbed after a key reception

It was Arkansas' seventeenth consecutive victory and it brought the Razorbacks an honor never before accorded the team from the land of the Ozarks. Two days later they were voted the No. 1 team in the nation in The Associated Press poll.

Brittenum's pass, setting up the final touchdown, was his tenth completion in nineteen attempts for 131 yards. His touchdown sneak marked the first time during the season that Texas had been scored upon on the ground. Crockett's climactic reception was his eighth of the game, for a total of 102 yards. Texas was determined to stop Harry Jones, and it did, limiting the ballcarrier to 31 yards. But Brittenum and Crockett got away.

Broyles admitted afterward that he had pilfered the effective pass pattern, used on the final drive, from Tulsa, a team he had beaten 20–12 in the second game of the season.

"Glenn Dobbs [Tulsa coach] ran us ragged with this pattern," the Arkansas coach said. "We've worked on it for three weeks, saving it for Texas."

That evening throughout Arkansas folk singers paid tribute to their football hero:

> *Now Jon Brittenum is happy callin' signals*
> *Behind the quickest line in the land.*
> *And anyone you ask in Razorback State*
> *Will tell you he's our quarterbackin' man . . .*
> *Jon Brittenum, he's our quarterbackin' man.*

Head coach of Arkansas, Frank Broyles   *Darrell Royal*

16

"Baby Bear" Turns on "Papa Bear"

COTTON BOWL: JANUARY 1, 1968

TEXAS A&M   20

ALABAMA   16

Up and down the sidelines in front of his bench, "Papa Bear" paced with quick, nervous steps. A checkered hat was pulled low over his eyes, the collar of a heavy wool jacket protecting his ears. He yelled at the players on the field. He barked instructions in sharp, penetrating tones as he maneuvered his personnel. He was obviously tense and on edge.

Across the way, the man they dubbed "Baby Bear," younger, hawk-faced, dapper in a white shirt, tie and houndstooth sport coat, was equally jumpy. He strode from one end of the field to the other. Occasionally, he grabbed a telephone, listened a moment and then called a man from the bench. He deployed his men as a grand master might move ivory figures on a chessboard — but with greater urgency.

The seventy-five thousand spectators in the stands and the millions watching on television almost could see and feel the mental sparks fly as teacher matched football wits with pupil in the Cotton Bowl game at Dallas on January 1, 1968.

Teacher-pupil battles in strategy were no novelty to Southwest football fans. Their pulses had thumped to thrilling games involving Bud Wilkinson of Oklahoma and his protégé, Darrell Royal, who went on to become head coach at Texas. There had been others, but none to whet the Texans' insatiable football appetite as much as this.

Paul (Bear) Bryant had created a legend as coach of Texas A&M for the four years from 1954 through 1957, as described in Chapter 9. One of the members of Bryant's A&M Junction Boys squad was Gene

Stallings, who later served seven years as assistant to Bryant at Alabama before returning to A&M as head coach in 1965.

"Gene is more like the Bear than the Bear himself," a contemporary commented. "If you closed your eyes, you couldn't tell which one was doing the coaching." Some started calling Stallings "Baby Bear."

The meeting of Bryant and his star pupil was cause for a reunion of the other members of the Junction Boys. You couldn't have kept them away with an injunction. John David Crow, ace halfback on the A&M team of a decade before, showed up on the Aggie side of the field with the gifted pass-catcher Bobby Joe Conrad. Crow acknowledged that he had mixed emotions. "You know how it is," he said apologetically to anyone who might have thought him disloyal to his former coach, "the young'un's trying to beat the old man. I know that's the way he'd want it." He gestured toward the Bear.

In the stands were Jack Pardee, Charlie Krueger and Roddy Osborne, other Stallings comrades and Bryant pupils, finding it difficult not to root for the younger man against the older. "It's all in the family," Krueger said. "I don't care who wins, really. I'd like to see a tie."

The underdog role, however, placed most of the sentiment behind Stallings and his Aggies. The Aggies, in a bumbling start, lost their first four games before pulling themselves together and finishing on a six-game winning streak that brought them the Southwest Conference title.

Alabama, on the other hand, had won eight games, had lost only to Tennessee and tied Florida State. The Crimson Tide, shooting for their third straight major bowl title, was ranked No. 7 nationally, and was favored by a touchdown.

Southwest fans were ecstatic over the match. Let the Rose Bowl have top-ranked Southern California and the great O. J. Simpson. Give the Sugar Bowl the nation's only unbeaten-untied team, Wyoming, and give the Orange Bowl the No. 2- and No. 3-ranked teams, Tennessee and Oklahoma. The Cotton Bowl had a natural.

It wasn't an ideal day for football. Sleet and cold rain had hit the city in the morning. At game time, the temperature was just above freezing — 34 degrees. The sky was the color of dirty dishwater. The field was damp and frozen.

Although the Aggies had distinguished themselves as a good defensive team — quick, tough, accustomed to hot pursuit and gang-tackling in true Bryant tradition — there was some question that the Texans would be able to contain the Alabama attack. The Tide had one of the nation's most effective passers and ballhandlers in Kenny (Snake) Stabler and an excellent receiver in end Dennis Homan.

Kenny Stabler of Alabama

David Chatwood, a speedy fullback, was hard to bring down on the ground.

Alabama didn't do much to erase these tensions when it lost the ball on a fumble the first time it gained possession and then came back to march 80 yards to a touchdown in ten easy plays. Stabler hit Homan with a 30-yard pass, and Chatwood galloped 14 yards during the drive. It appeared that the Aggie defense might have halted the push when the Tide found itself with a fourth down and two at the 10-yard line. Here Stabler cagily went into a long count, pulled the eager Aggies offside and got a first down at the five. On second down, after a two-yard line play, Stabler faked to tailback Ed Morgan and wiggled over the goal line. Steve Davis kicked the extra point and Alabama led, 7–0.

Stallings was not without tricks himself. The Aggies had proved themserves a strong running team and the Crimson Tide bunched the defense to stop the Aggies up the middle. The Aggies surprisingly came out throwing the ball.

A minute and a half after Alabama had put the first score on the board, the Aggies got a break when Tommy Maxwell intercepted a Stabler pass — the first of three they were to swipe during the afternoon — and gave A&M the ball at the Alabama 43.

The Aggies' quarterback Edd Hargett, destined to be voted the outstanding player of the game, shook up the Tide immediately by con-

Edd Hargett,
Aggie quarterback

necting on a 28-yard pass to split end Barney Harris. Harris was playing with a heavy heart. On the Saturday night before the Monday game his father had died in San Antonio after a long illness. Barney flew home to attend the funeral and then, at the urging of his family, rushed back, arriving in Dallas just before the kickoff.

The pass put the ball on Alabama's 15-yard line. Larry Stegent picked up two yards through the middle and, after a Hargett-to-Harris pass had failed, snared a 13-yard pass from Hargett for the score. Bobby Riggs's kick made it 7–7.

On the first play of the second quarter, Alabama went ahead 10–7 when Steve Davis kicked a 36-yard field goal, the second longest ever booted in the Cotton Bowl.

The two teams battled doggedly — without much quarter given on either side — through most of the period. Then, just before the half, Alabama made another of its rare mistakes and A&M was there to take advantage of it. The Tide was moving when Stabler shot a 10-yard pass to Perry Willis, who grabbed the ball on the Aggie 34 only to be jarred by two A&M tacklers. The ball squirted from his arms and the Aggies' Jim Piper pounced on it.

Hargett proceeded to take the Texans 56 yards in eight plays for a go-ahead touchdown. Again it was Hargett's pinpoint passing which moved the team. The quarterback passed 17 yards to Tommy Maxwell,

21 yards to Tom Buckman and 14 yards to Stegent. Stegent, a rangy sophomore, made a spectacular stab at the ball. He caught it with one hand, bobbled it momentarily, then brought it to his chest, falling to the ground at the seven. On the next play, Hargett passed to Maxwell in the end zone for the score. Riggs, who had kicked 15 of 18 conversion tries during the year, missed. The ball hit the goalposts and veered wide, but the Aggies led, 13–10.

Coming back onto the field after intermission, Alabama was geared to stop Hargett's passing. The A&M quarterback had crossed up the Tide by throwing the ball twenty-two times in the opening half, gaining only twelve yards on the ground. Now Bear Bryant and his team were in for another jolt. Instead of passing, Hargett decided to go to his infantry. Tossing only two passes in the last half in an abrupt shift in

Aggie tailback, Larry Stegent breaks into the end zone on a pass play from Hargett

offensive strategy, Hargett went to ball control with the shifty Stegent and his six-two, 210-pound churning fullback Wendell Housley.

Midway into the third period, the Aggies got the ball at their own 49 after a short 28-yard punt by Davis. Hargett threw only one pass, a 10-yarder, to Harris, and the rest of the time stayed on the ground. Housley smashed off tackle for 13 yards and later broke loose for 20 yards and a touchdown. A half-dozen Alabama white shirts got hands on him but he shook loose and went all the way. Riggs got his sights back and kicked the extra point for a 20–10 A&M lead.

No one in the stands and no one on the Aggie side of the field expected Alabama to toss in the towel at this stage, and Alabama didn't. With the snap-back, never-say-die attitude that is the trademark of Bryant teams, the Tide surged ahead for 83 yards in nine plays. Stabler passed 19 yards to Danny Ford and 22 to Homan to get into scoring

Hargett under fire gets good protection: Mike Ford (No. 81) is about to be dropped by an Aggie lineman

position, and then he cut over tackle himself for the final seven yards and the score.

With the score now 20–16 in favor of the Aggies, Bryant, never one to settle for a tie, decided to go for two points instead of one, putting his team in a position to win with a field goal. The maneuver failed. Fullback Dave Chatwood was stacked up in the middle of the line.

"In a situation like this, we usually go for the pass-run option," Bryant recalled later. "But A&M surprised us and came out with a spread instead of a tight defense. So at the last minute we decided to try a sneak over the center of the line. It wasn't until afterward that I learned the Aggies had only ten men on the field at the time — through an oversight — and a pass probably would have worked."

It made no difference. There were only sixteen seconds left in the third period when Alabama scored the final points of the game. The last period proved to be a scoreless — though dramatic — standoff.

In the closing stages, it was a battle of rugged, hard-hitting defenses. Every time one team made a gesture, it was smothered and forced to punt. The two kept wrestling for a break. During this infighting, one player stood out above the rest. He was Bill Hobbs, A&M linebacker. Hobbs was credited with seven tackles and seven assists and voted the outstanding lineman in the game. Finally, with four minutes to play, the Crimson Tide roused itself for one big, last-gasp effort. Starting at its own 13, Alabama came out in single wing formation, surprising Aggie defenders who had not seen the lineup on their scouting films and were caught totally unprepared. From his deep position, Stabler began a passing attack, mostly short shots to Dennis Homan, with some line dashes by Chatwood. Once during the drive, Stabler picked up only six yards on a pass to Homan when 11 were needed on fourth down, but the Aggies drew a 15-yard penalty for holding. The Alabama drive stayed alive.

Tension mounted as the Tide, racing the clock, moved past midfield into A&M territory. There was a loud gasp from the fans — and a sigh from the Aggie rooters — when Homan, in the clear, let a pass slip through his fingers on the Aggie 19.

With 22 seconds remaining, Stabler cut loose another long, desperation pass. Curley Hallman, A&M defensive back who went to high school in Tuscaloosa, Alabama, intercepted on his own 36. That was the game. The Aggies held until time ran out.

In the post-game commotion, Bear Bryant walked across the field to congratulate his former pupil, Stallings. They met at the 40-yard line. The tall, bull-strong Bryant — in a moment of impulse — grabbed the smiling Stallings by the legs and hoisted him to his shoulders, in the tradition of football victories.

"I was stunned," Stallings said later. "I didn't know what to make of it."

"It was just a sudden thought," Bryant said. "The kid did a great coaching job. It was coaching that won the game. If Stallings had coached Alabama, Alabama would have won."

Most observers felt Bryant was being overly gracious. The Alabama team violated one of Bryant's strongest tenets: "Keep from losing the game before you try to win it." The pendulum of the game swung on mistakes. Alabama beat A&M in the statistics, 14 first downs to 13, 135 rushing yards to 114, and 179 passing yards to 143. But the Tide had three passes stolen and lost two fumbles.

"A coach is responsible for his team's mistakes," Bryant insisted. "If I'd coached these boys well, they wouldn't have made these mistakes."

In the A&M dressing room, cries went up: "Stallings for President!"

"Not me," said Gene, the victorious Baby Bear. "I like my job better."

Paul (Bear) Bryant lifts pupil and winning Texas A&M coach Gene Stallings into the air